TRANG COMMUNICATIONS/CHARISMA HOUSE/SILOAM/
LINE products are available at special quantity discounts for
urchases for sales promotions, premiums, fund-raising, and
ional needs. For details, write Strang Communications/Cha-
House/Siloam/FrontLine, 600 Rinehart Road, Lake Mary,
a 32746, or telephone (407) 333-0600.

EVER TOO LATE by Zachery Tims
hed by Charisma House
ng Company
nehart Road
Mary, Florida 32746
charismahouse.com

s otherwise indicated, Scripture quotations are taken from
King James Version of the Bible. Copyright © 1979, 1980, 1982
omas Nelson, Inc., publishers. Used by permission.

ture quotations marked ESV are from The Holy Bible, English
ard Version. Copyright © 2001, Crossway Bibles, a division of
News Publishers. Used by permission. All rights reserved.

ture quotations marked KJV are from the King James Version of
ible.

ture quotations marked NIV are from the Holy Bible, New
national Version. Copyright © 1973, 1978, 1984, International
Society. Used by permission.

er design by John Hamilton Design
          www.johnhamiltondesign.com

It's Neve
Too L

Zachery Tims

Charisma
HOUSE
A STRANG COMPANY

Most

FRON

bulk

educa

risma

Flori

IT'S

Publi

A Str

600 F

Lake

www

This

in a

elect

prior

Unit

Unle

New

by T

Scri

Stan

God

Scri

the

Scri

Inte

Bib

Cov

Library of Congress Cataloging-in-Publication Data

Tims, Zachery.
  It's never too late / Zachery Tims.
     p. cm.
  ISBN 1-59185-980-8 (hardback)
  1. Tims, Zachery. 2. Clergy--Biography. 3. Christian biography. 4.
Christian life. I. Title.
  BR1725.T555A3 2006
  277.3'082092--dc22
  [B]
                           2006020217

First edition

06 07 08 09 10 — 987654321
Printed in the United States of America

This book is dedicated to all those who have fallen into darkness and cannot see the light at the end of the tunnel; to all those who feel as if they have hit rock bottom with no way of getting up. I have written this book to encourage you not to give up, for there is still hope. When I think of you, I think of me. You are my inspiration. I experienced the power of God that can and will change your life.

This book is written by a man who has been blessed to receive many chances through the grace of God's unconditional love. I have come back from the dead with a message for you. Even when everyone looks at you and sees a failure, God sees beyond your mistakes, and He sees your potential. Don't you dare give up!

Please reach up, because He's reaching down, ready to pull you out of the pit where you may be struggling . . . *It's Never Too Late.*

Acknowledgment

FIRST OF ALL, I want to thank the Lord Jesus Christ for saving me from me and allowing my life to become a testimony of His goodness and mercy, letting others know that God is in the recycling business and can change a messed-up life and make it beautiful.

I want to express my gratitude to my wife, Riva, and our children for your love and support and for sharing me with the world. I also want to acknowledge the New Destiny Christian Center family and staff for your encouragement and compassion for me to do all that God has assigned.

Thank you, Mr. Stephen Strang, for being an integral part of putting this testimony of hope into the hands of so many people who have the hopeless belief that it is too late. You and your wife, Joy, are a real blessing to the body of Christ.

I also want to say thank you to the following:

- Dr. Miles Monroe, for inspiring me with vision to write this book. Your revelation on potential and the kingdom has been a vehicle in elevating my ministry and my personal life.

- Bishop T. D. Jakes, for challenging me to go beyond where I thought I could go by allowing me to "see" the world with different eyes. It takes a well-balanced man to realize that everything is not what it seems.

- Pastor Benny Hinn, for global vision to bring the world to the saving knowledge of Jesus Christ. Thanks for the opportunity for me to travel every continent and see God's amazing power to deliver and set free those who were held captive.

- Bishop Randy and Pastor Paula White, for your unconditional love and support. Thank you for refusing to let me think small, for helping me to see outside the four walls of the church, and for continually stretching me to believe God for the supernatural.

- Valerie Lowe, for making yourself available to ensure a smooth process. And my thanks to Rick Killian for your assistance in the preparation of the manuscript.

- Rená Jones, for operating in the spirit of excellence while staying on top of all of the edits and meeting the deadlines for this manuscript. Thank you, Elder Cherie, for your comments and your assistance.

Contents

—Part Four—
Sow the Way You Want to Go

—Part Five—
Live From the Fruit of Your Gifts;
Let God Establish Your Calling

Introduction

IFE IS LIKE a puzzle. We work at it, focusing on one individual piece at time, working to finish one section of the puzzle at a time. Most people who have had some experience putting puzzles together will start with the corners and the edges, working to develop the outline of the whole. Then they will focus on developing different areas on the inside that are easier first—this part is water, so all these blue pieces go there; these are sky pieces; these look like trees; and so forth. They can check the cover of the box to approximate where the pieces should go—or else guess at what pieces they should be looking for—to fill in the section they are focusing on at that moment in time.

Unlike with a puzzle, however, real life doesn't come with a picture on the cover of the box—we don't know the totality, the total sum of our lives. We only know one section or piece at a time, but we are still expected to understand exactly where it goes. Without the picture on the box, we tend to make long-term, life-changing decisions based only on a couple of pieces of the puzzle at a time. It may not be until we look back years later, when we know more of what that picture should look like, that we realize we made the right decisions or that we forced some of our pieces into the wrong place.

Destiny is like that picture on the box. The problem is that most of us never get that full view of our lives, so we make incomplete decisions. When I was young, I really messed up some of my pieces because I didn't know there was a "picture on the box" out there for me. All I knew is what I saw around me and whether my edge aligned with someone else's or not. I did everything I knew to fit in. As a result, I fell in with the wrong crowd, did the wrong things, and was on the wrong road to my future. Had there not been a major intervention by God—the One who not only knew the picture on my box but also painted it—I would probably have been dead before the age of twenty.

I learned another valuable analogy along the way: life is like writing a book. Books have lots of chapters, and sometimes they even come in volumes. The only difference is that we can't rewrite the past; we can only choose to write a better present in hope of it leading to a greater future. When you are in the midst of a bad chapter, the answer is not to throw the book away, but to close one chapter and start another one. Sometimes it may even be time to close one volume and start on a completely different one! But whatever you do, don't throw the entire book away! You just need to go to a new page and start fresh from there.

There are two things I have learned and want you to see in these analogies:

1. You are not a mistake: there is a plan and a purpose—a "picture on the box" or destiny—for each of us.

2. It is never too late to start over better than before.

In the following pages, you will find out about some of the chapters in my life and what I learned from them. It is my hope that what I learned can help you also.

Early in my life I had no idea that there might be a bigger picture for me, so being young and insecure, I latched onto the examples of drug dealers and gangbangers in the hood that were available to me. It was years before I discovered that they had only been there to try to kill me, as they did six of my friends who were murdered during the time I was with the gangs. I didn't know it wasn't too late for me to start a new chapter of my life either, so the first time I slipped up after returning home from detention for possession and assault, I got right back into the drug scene again. It led me, once again, into an addiction that was aimed at destroying me.

But today I am not dead, nor am I strung out and in bondage to some addiction. Not only did I survive, but through the process I also learned to thrive!

I want you to know that you can, too.

It's never too late!

I have pulled together this book of my life story not because I am some great guy, but because I have a great God who knows where all the pieces of your life should go and wants to help you put it together. I want you to be able to learn from what I went through without going through it yourself, and get the keys you need to live the most fulfilling life you can. I want you to realize that the best is still ahead for you and that there are changes you can still make to realize your dreams. I want you to always remember, no matter what happens—

It's never too late!

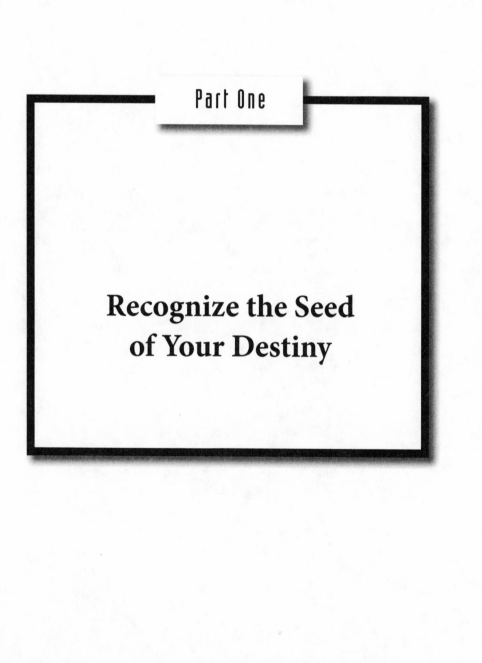

Part One

Recognize the Seed
of Your Destiny

One

Before You Were Born, God Put a Plan and Purpose in Your Heart

"For I know the plans I have for you," declares the LORD, "plans to prosper you and not to harm you, plans to give you hope and a future."

—*Jeremiah 29:11, NIV*

I F YOU HAD seen me in the Baltimore projects at the age of twelve, you would have never known I had a God-given destiny. There's no way I had any clue about it. I was just a hungry young kid being raised by a single mom. But I had an eye for more in life. I knew I was looking for something. I also knew I was going to be somebody. The problem was that I discovered an *identity* long before

1

I had any clue about *destiny*—and that identity was set to kill me and squash my destiny before I even knew I had one.

My father and mother were divorced when I was about nine years old, and my mother and I moved into a nice little rental townhouse in northeast Baltimore. Those townhouses are no longer there. They were torn down a few years back, and new homes were built on the property.

Being new and an only child, I found it hard to relate to others in the immediate area. The neighborhood looked and seemed like a good lower-middle-, upper-poor-class neighborhood on the surface, but lurking less than a half mile away were the low-income units of the Surrel Apartments. All you needed to do was walk through a few alleyways and across a field, and you would find yourself in the midst of rundown, government-assisted housing that was filled with single mothers who had more children than they could handle. Drug dealers thrived here, so there were lots of addicts, mothers and children alike.

My father was a detective with the Baltimore Police Department, but he always spent more time in the bar after hours than he ever did at home, even after he remarried a few years later. He was extremely charismatic and popular among his colleagues, as well as the life of the party at whatever bar he hung out at. For a while, he even owned a restaurant above a bar in town that prospered for a time because he was so well known and liked by those who came to eat there.

My mother was a wonderfully kind and loving woman who didn't know anything more than what she had learned growing up in the neighborhoods of Baltimore. During the week she would work hard to provide for us and then go out to clubs on Friday nights, where she'd drink and dance to unwind and meet men. She just didn't know any other type of life. She took me to church maybe half a dozen times as I grew up, on Christmas, Easter, or something, but that is as close as we ever got to knowing anything about God. Yet she always had a heart that wanted to do good, and she was a giving person. If you needed a ride home, she'd give you a ride home; if you needed five dollars, she'd give you five dollars; and if you needed hundred dollars and she had it, she'd give you a hundred dollars.

Despite being a single parent, my mother worked hard enough to send me to private school. I attended St. Thomas Moore Elementary School as a seventh and eighth grader, and then Archbishop Curley High School as a ninth and tenth grader. Believe it or not, I was an honor student. My mother always made sure I looked good in my school uniform. Both schools were all-boys' schools. I don't remember anything they taught me about God that ever made any kind of impact on me, even though we regularly had to attend Mass as part of our schooling. It was just a joke to me. My friends and I would whisper through it or do anything other than pay attention. I definitely had no concept of the power of God, who Jesus Christ really was, or what that meant to me personally.

What did make an impression on me, however, were the guys I would see hanging around on the streets as I walked home or ran errands for my mom. I'd see them roaming around in groups or hanging out on one particular corner of the shopping center near an arcade. At first they just seemed part of the neighborhood, like a statue in a park or something. But the guys roaming the streets in expensive puff NFL or NBA coats, lambskin jackets, Baltimore puff leathers, designer jeans, and Air Jordans sort of stuck out above the rest. After a while they started to make an impression on me. They seemed to have it together despite the poverty around them. They had nice clothes, seemed friendly, and always seemed to have money to spend.

I had some cousins in the area who were more than ten years older than I was, so I got into the habit of hanging out with an older crowd. They were great to be around and accepted me. Because of this, it was easier to hang with these guys on the corner near the arcade. They were friendly, though they were cool about it. It felt good just to stand there with them and not be chased off. They let me and my friends join their conversations as if we had always been there. They asked me about my school and where I lived. They asked me about my family. It made me feel pretty good to be standing with them there, like I was cool and had it together just like I thought they did. For a young kid, especially one with no father at home, it was the closest thing to an image of success I had ever seen.

I remember it being the NCAA basketball tournament when most of the local attention was on the upcoming game between Georgetown and Virginia—the key matchup being Patrick Ewing vs. Ralph Sampson. Trying to be cool and fit in, I asked Marcus, one of the older guys—he was twenty-something—to go into the liquor store and buy me a "forty"—what we called the 40-ounce beers they sold—so that I would have it to watch the game the next night. He agreed, and when he came back he offered me a joint to go with it. He told me, "Here, take this too, and enjoy the game." To be honest, I think those were really the first affirming words I had ever heard from someone I looked up to in my life other than my mother or family. I didn't miss the subtlety of what this suggested—that I was "in" and accepted in his crowd. I felt about ten feet tall.

I snuck the beer and joint into my room that night, opened my window to try to cover the smell, lit that joint, and took a few puffs. I have to admit, though, I got more of a charge out of Marcus giving it to me than I actually did out of smoking it. Somehow I think my body knew I didn't need it, but my head was all caught up with my desire to be identified with this group of guys. I was becoming socially addicted. It was as if I stepped through a doorway that night, though it had very little to do with the joint. Before I had been on the *outside*; now I was *in*. It is sad to say, but I had nothing else in my life at this point that made me feel worth anything, and because of that low self-esteem and lack of purpose in my life, when Marcus offered me even a little bit of affirmation, I jumped to be part of whatever he was into.

After that, my cousins and I began hanging out with this crew pretty often in our spare time, especially after school and before my mom got home. Marcus—who had given me the joint—started introducing me to people from the neighborhood, most of whom where gang members, drug dealers, druggies, or girls who hung out with them. My mother thought I was there playing arcade games, but I was actually building unhealthy relationships with all the wrong people in the neighborhood.

Often, the guys would go over to the Goodnow Hill Apartments, where there were laundry rooms on the first floor that were always open. We would drink and smoke, and the guys would start singing old songs—and their singing wasn't half bad. Hanging out with these guys made me feel older. Eventually I noticed that even though these guys never worked, they always had new stylish street wear on. When the women came by, they all knew these guys by name. Some of the guys would break off from the rest of us and talk with the girls one-on-one or in small groups, making arrangements to meet up later and party at somebody's pad later that night. This intrigued me; I didn't want to work, but I sure wanted all the nice things and attention from the girls they had.

It was around this time that my mother started losing complete control of me. I was so cocky that I just started doing whatever I wanted to even though she had told me just the opposite. She was doing the best she could, but with no man in my everyday life—I only stayed with my father every once in a while—I grew more and more reckless. In fact, one time when I was at my dad's, I was baby-sitting my four-year-old stepbrother, and there was some party or something that I wanted to be at, so I just left him there alone in the house! In the end, nothing happened to him, but I certainly caught it from my father when I got back. I had no respect regarding what either of my parents said, which just drove me deeper into the life I found on the streets and hanging out with the gang.

Then one day while I was hanging with the guys, Marcus called me over: "Hey Zach, do me a favor?"

My eyes must have lit up. "What do you need?"

"Well, look, I need to get some stuff to a guy. Down that alley behind the big Dumpster there is a sack with some little bags in it. Could you get one of these and take it to a guy in the apartments across the street for me?"

I nodded.

Now I was no dummy. I knew it was marijuana in the bag and that these guys had access to drugs, because they talked about them from time to time. I knew all of them smoked a little pot. "No big deal. We just do it to relax," they'd say. Some even did cocaine when partying with girls, but I didn't say anything about it because I wanted to fit in.

So, after he had given me the last of the instructions, I walked off, slow and cool like he had told me to. I was just supposed to look like a kid walking home from school. I am sure the school uniform helped.

When I was sure no one was looking, I ducked into the alley to find his stash. The Dumpster stank of rotting food, and the alley was dark in the shadows of the buildings. It took me a couple of minutes to find Marcus's bag, which was well hidden. But when I did, I quickly pulled out one of the plastic bags of grass and stashed it in my inside coat pocket. Then I headed back into the street as cool as I could play it.

I was anything but cool on the inside, though. My heart was racing, and I did my best to keep my steps even and not get myself noticed. I made my way across the street to the dirty, brick building with the right number. As I eased myself inside, I felt a little more protected for a moment, but this place was much more rundown than where I lived, and I grew more anxious as I made my way up the stairs to each new floor. Finally I found the correct apartment number and knocked.

I heard some rumbling behind the door, but it didn't open. "Who's there?" The voice sounded tired and a little hoarse.

"Marcus sent me," I said.

The door rattled slowly and opened a crack. I could see it was still chained shut. The guy's eyes searched the halls over my head before looking at me. "Where is it?" he said gruffly.

"You got Marcus's money?" I asked.

"Sure," he said, and I could see him reach for his wallet and pull out some bills. He held out the wad, I pulled the plastic bag from my coat, and we made the exchange. My heart was racing faster than ever. "Uh, thanks," he said, and shut the door. I could hear it latching again as I made my way back to the stairs.

Marcus's money felt hot in my pocket. I hadn't even counted it, so I am sure it felt like much more than it actually was. When I got back to Marcus and handed him the money, he counted it, and then grinned at me. "Good job, kid. You're a real pro," he said, then he added that small wad of bills to a much larger one he pulled from his pocket. He patted me on the back, and we headed back to stand with the others. Later he slipped me another joint for my help.

I can't tell you what if felt like to have Marcus's words of praise. I had never experienced anything like it before in my life, and I didn't want it to stop.

So, slowly I began to run these errands more often. As a reward, they started giving me more free marijuana, then handed down some sportswear, and eventually there was some money. I was moving up the ladder, and the guys started to tell me more. I soon learned that all of these guys hanging on the corner not only smoked marijuana and sniffed cocaine from time to time, but they also sold it. They told me that while they didn't use heavy drugs, they did sell them for the extra cash. They said they steered clear of the big stuff themselves as it was too addicting, and they didn't want to mess with it. They just did the "safe, party drugs," they said.

To a young kid who didn't know anything, that seemed smart. It was so subtle. I had hung around with them so long and had been introduced to all of this so slowly that it all seemed natural and normal. As far as I was concerned, they knew what they were doing—they were making money, and they enjoyed life like no one I had ever met. Plus they were so cool to me—it was hard in those early days to see it as the trap it really was.

Today, it is obvious to me now that I was reaching and crying out for something at that time and that these were the only guys answering that cry. It didn't really seem that I was dealing drugs so much as I was doing these guys—my friends—a favor. As we said in the hood, they were my "ace boon coon"—buddies, brothers, friends—and every time I did them a favor, they trusted me more, and I belonged more. I saw what they had and wanted it, so I figured if I did what they did, I could get it, too. Eventually I asked one of the guys if he would hook me up with my own stuff to sell, and he agreed.

Now I had a stash to send other kids after. I got hooked on selling at that point. I got hooked on the money. I had gone from being a runner to a lieutenant, and I was now doing my own thing—just like them. I was buying whole packages, hanging out on the corners, and having others want to hang out with me. The younger boys were now my runners, and, in my mind, I was just like the older guys who I thought were my friends. And even though I was really young, women—not just teenage girls, but *women*—started paying attention to me. I thought I was making it with style.

By the time I was thirteen, I was making $1,000 a week, or close to it. I was popular, I had nice clothes, and I bought my first big gold rope chain to wear. I was making easy money, my rep was growing, and I had the look of the identity that had first drawn me to these guys. It was like a dream, because I idealized this foolishness. I was blind and couldn't see the trap that was being set. As far as I was concerned, I could do anything I wanted to do. No one, not even my mother, could stop me from walking straight into the devil's trap. I was so deceived. I had bought into this artificial world, which had been carefully and meticulously planned to take me out. I was getting everything I felt I was supposed to have, but it was all on the devil's terms, and because of that, he was getting ready to bring it all crashing down around my head.

I had traded the destiny calling in my heart for an identity that had been carefully developed to draw me in. As the seed of my destiny was growing in me, calling for more than the hood in Baltimore had to offer, the gangs and drug dealers were there to distract me from it and to make me think they had it all. This pseudo success seemed to answer the destiny calling inside of me, even though it was a cheap counterfeit of my true destiny. These gang members lived a life where, as far as I could tell as a young teen, they had everything they wanted and could fulfill their every desire. What more could the world possibly have to offer?

What I didn't realize is that what I needed—and what we all need—is something more than the world has to offer.

Don't Confuse an External Identity With Your God-given Destiny

According to the *American Heritage Dictionary*, one of the meanings of *identity* is "the quality or condition of being exactly the same as something else." It is something outside of you that you can see, and you try to match it in every aspect of its external appearance. In other words, it is striving to be a copy of someone or something else—whether that image be a rapper, a gang member, a father, a drug dealer, or a sports hero. It is something you latch onto with your eyes, and unconsciously assert, *That is what I want to be like. That is the crowd I want to fit in with.* In this sense, identity is accepting the future the world wants you to have, the future that someone else has chosen for you. It becomes a way for you to be controlled and kept from ever really making any positive difference in the world or living any kind of a fulfilling life.

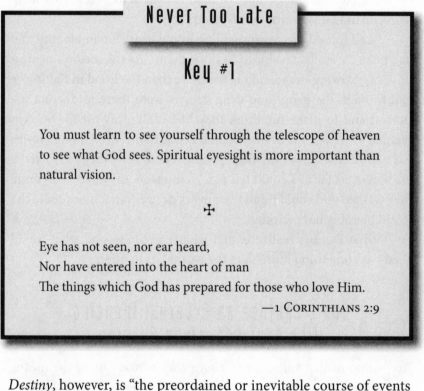

Never Too Late

Key #1

You must learn to see yourself through the telescope of heaven to see what God sees. Spiritual eyesight is more important than natural vision.

✝

Eye has not seen, nor ear heard,
Nor have entered into the heart of man
The things which God has prepared for those who love Him.
—1 CORINTHIANS 2:9

Destiny, however, is "the preordained or inevitable course of events considered as something beyond the power or control of man." In other words, destiny is the plan that God has for your life and your fulfillment. It is the plan for your life He is trying to work through you so that you can truly be all you can be. It is your purpose for being on this earth, and without it you will never really be happy.

You need to realize that God put that destiny inside of you before you were even born. From your childhood, destiny begins to call to you and draw you toward the things and purposes God wants for you. Here is how God described Jeremiah's destiny to him:

> Before I formed you in the womb I knew you;
> Before you were born I sanctified you;
> I ordained you a prophet to the nations.
>
> —JEREMIAH 1:5

For some, destiny is a call to help others that may someday result in that person becoming a social worker, a doctor, a missionary, an aid worker in a foreign country, or any number of other helping occupations. You may feel a call to art, and make music that refreshes and energizes others, write poetry that inspires, create films or paintings that open truth to our culture, write great novels that help people unlock the passions of their heart, or any number of other things artists do. You may be called to business, politics, education, ministry, science, technical work, or some other area of life. Whatever it is, from the time you were conceived God already had a unique plan for you to live a fulfilled and purposeful life. He took that plan in seed form and planted it in your heart so that it could grow and develop as you grew and developed from a child into a teenager and into an adult.

The problem is...*the devil has a destiny for your life as well.* For every good and worthwhile calling God has, the world has a temporarily satisfying but ultimately empty and destructive counterfeit. He wants to see you live a miserable, defeated, worthless life that not only hurts you but also hurts every other life you touch. I know, because I've been there. While hooking up with those drug dealers seemed so good as a boy, it wasn't too many years before the devil's plan tried to kill me, or, short of that, leave me so empty and strung out that I was hardly living at all.

It's so important for you to realize that the counterfeit identity, which always looks so much easier, so much more readily available, so much more appealing, and so well fitted to the call of destiny in your heart, will end by taking you far away from your true destiny and what God wants to accomplish in your life. Today I believe that from my mother's womb God was calling me to be a businessman, to live a full and prosperous life helping others, to be a leader in my community, and, eventually, to be a pastor spreading God's Word and helping others live out the destinies He has called them to. Yet when I was a young boy, the devil presented me with the counterfeit identity of dealing drugs. It had most of the elements of business without the hard work or responsibilities. It had the image of success and wealth I felt my future held for me. It offered the "community leadership" of being in a gang and having others look up to me. It even had a *gospel* of its own to spread to everyone I touched: "Life is hard, and you will never get ahead, so just take these drugs, and it won't seem so painful and empty for a little while." It had every element I felt called to, but instead of leading to life, it ministered death to everyone I met.

The Bible is full of examples of this same thing. When Joseph was a seventeen-year-old lad, God gave him a dream that he would be a leader of his people, but instead, Joseph used that dream to lord himself over his brothers to the point that they wanted to kill him. God gave Moses the vision that he would one day free the Hebrew people from the chains of Egypt, and as a result, he murdered a man in cold blood, thinking it was by his own hand that this deliverance would come. Even Paul said that he had been called and separated from his mother's womb to be a religious leader, but he accepted legalism instead of grace and started his ministry persecuting and killing the followers of Jesus—the same people God had called him to lead into a greater understanding of the love of God. (See Galatians 1:15–16.)

God Doesn't See You as a Failure

The counterfeit identities of the world always appeal to the call of our destinies, yet always end in doing the exact opposite. Even though they seem so alike at the beginning, instead of bringing life, the world's fulfillment brings death; instead of light, it brings darkness; instead of humility and service to others, false identity brings pride and the desire to dominate. Such identities are there to attract us like moths to a flame—the beginning seems so bright, but in the end, we crash into ashes.

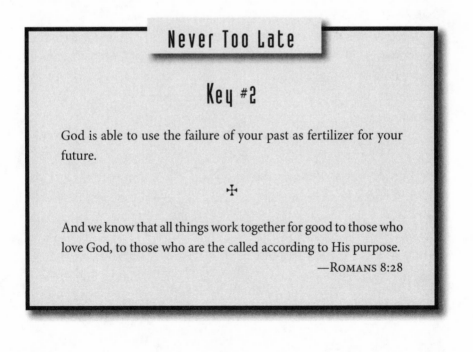

Never Too Late

Key #2

God is able to use the failure of your past as fertilizer for your future.

✠

And we know that all things work together for good to those who love God, to those who are the called according to His purpose.

—ROMANS 8:28

Yet despite all of this, there is something else you really need to understand: No matter where you are in life—you could be a young kid, a high-school dropout, a prison inmate at thirty-five, a retiree, or whatever—when God looks at you, He doesn't see a failure or a victim of "identity crisis." He sees your destiny fulfilled in you. He doesn't see sin; He sees salvation. He doesn't see poverty; He sees true riches. He doesn't see weaknesses; He sees supernatural ability. Where others see wilderness, God sees a path to the promised land. All you have to do to move into the destiny God has for you is to figure out how to get from where you are now to the fulfilled destiny God already sees in you.

Two

Don't Let an Identity Destroy Your Destiny

> Be sober, be vigilant; because your adversary the devil walks about like a roaring lion, seeking whom he may devour.
>
> —*1 Peter 5:8*

B Y THE TIME I was fourteen years old, I had seen many of my friends get strung out, locked up, and, for some, even murdered. But to me this was all just a part of the hustle and flow—you lose a gang member, and you raise up another—and I was too far in it to pull out. I wasn't addicted to the drugs, but I had become addicted to being cool, being in, and being accepted by these hoodlums, gangbangers, and womanizers. After all, I was one of them.

Being in a gang was tough, but at the same time it fed my ego. In a way, the danger just made it more attractive. You had your crew, and there was respect for it because it held a territory it defended to the death. There were several street corners in the area that we considered "our turf," and we did quite a lucrative business selling from them. In my mind we had it going on. Like in the movies, we were a band of brothers fighting invaders and having each other's backs against attacks that could come at any time.

Though we sold a lot in the projects, we also sold to whoever would pull up on the corners that we knew. We had clients from all over the area who had jobs and lived in nice homes, blue collar and white collar alike. Some would even pull up in Cadillacs or BMWs to get their stuff. It meant a steady flow of cash, which corrupted me as much as the company I was keeping. Having a lot of money will do funny things to your head if you are not living for anything bigger than yourself.

By this time, I was dealing more and more and making more and more money. In fact, I began making more money than some of the guys that were there before me. I was the youngest in the group, but it didn't seem to matter. I even began living with a woman in the projects who was twenty-one years old. I had told her I was older, but I'm sure she knew I was young. I was cool, and people liked me—and I liked being liked.

Slowly my "little corner market" began to suck away what little focus I had left for school. I cut classes and showed up only when I had drug deals to make. I was out of control. In my mind, it was a 24/7 party. We slept during the day, ran during the evening, and partied from midnight until dawn.

Around this time, I also started carrying a gun. To tell you the truth, I had never even fired it, but I started carrying it because it was part of the identity I had adopted. I showed it to the other guys, and they thought I was tougher for it. My rep was growing. I was becoming increasingly successful. In fact, I was starting to make some of the other guys jealous. As I climbed this demented ladder of "success," somehow I created an enemy in a guy I'd considered to be a friend and partner. I will call him Tony.

Tony was somewhere in his late twenties, and I thought he was one of my closest friends in our gang. We hung out together all the time, and he knew where I kept all of my stuff. For a time, we had even dated two girls who were sisters. It seemed like we were family.

Then one day while he and I and some others were messing around in the basement of my house with some girls while my mom was at work, Tony snuck over and opened the deadbolt on the basement door when I wasn't paying attention. Later he came back and stole everything: my stash, my money, and even an extra gun I had hidden with it. I don't think he wanted the stuff so much as to take me down a few notches. He didn't want some stupid high-school kid showing him up with everyone else in the hood.

I don't think I would ever have figured out he was the one except that he started bragging about it to all the other guys. I don't think he cared if it got back to me; in fact, he probably wanted me to know just to put me down more. What was I going to do anyway? I was just a kid after all, right?

What probably added to his thinking is that I had never been a violent guy or any kind of fighter. In my few years with the others I had never been in a fight, and I'm sure if I had, I would have lost. I was a skinny kid, and I really didn't care about anything enough to fight someone over it. I was just a smart kid who was good with numbers and in it for the business. I knew if I lost money, I could always find a way to earn it back with my head and not my fists.

But when Tony started bragging about "stealing Zach's stuff," something in me snapped. He was bigger than me, older than me, and more experienced than me in every aspect, but I wanted to shut him up. It was crazy in a demonic kind of way, and every time I thought about him, all I heard in my head was, *Kill him! Kill him!*

It is strange how twisted your mind can get when you start following the world's ways, especially when you are just a teenager and think you are invincible. You have no concept of ever facing consequences for your actions; you just do what you feel like doing without ever thinking about what might happen. When I started selling drugs, I never thought about being arrested or shot at or robbed, only that I was going to fit in with the guys on the corner if I did what they did. It is amazing how quickly you can go from doing the slightest wrong things, like running packages for a friend, to wanting to kill someone because he was damaging your rep. Truthfully, at the time, I saw nothing wrong with killing Tony. Gang shootings were commonplace and just went with the turf. It was part of the identity, and I was completely fooled. The devil had me square in his sights.

So I called Tony on the phone. "Man, we need to meet and settle this. Word is you took my stuff—that you been bragging all over that I'm just a kid. That ain't right, man."

Tony didn't seem to care, though, and he wouldn't admit it. "I'm ready! I didn't take your stuff. But if you want to get it on, let's get it on."

I asked him to meet me on a street near where I lived. I wasn't even smart enough to do it far from my home, and Tony was also deceived enough to come and meet me. I think he must have thought we were going to get into a fistfight or something, and being bigger and older than I was, it gave him another chance to teach me a lesson. Or maybe he didn't realize I had another gun, because he had stolen the .38 I kept with my stash. Maybe he figured I would never try anything since we were going to meet in broad daylight, or that since I was so young I wouldn't have the guts to use a gun or a knife. I don't know, but whatever he thought, I had no intention of letting him get close enough to even touch me.

It doesn't take any courage to pull a trigger. I remember waiting for him that afternoon, watching to see that nobody was around, and then getting jumpy when I saw him round the corner. All I could hear were those voices in my head saying, *Kill him! Kill him!* In a blur of emotion, when he was still about ten yards away, I panicked, pulled the gun from my pocket, and started firing. As soon as he saw the gun, he turned to run, but it was too late. Within seconds I had emptied all six shots without even aiming, but I'd intended with every one of them to end his life.

As soon as my squeezing of the trigger started sounding hollow on empty rounds, I cut and ran without looking back. The thoughts in my head of *Kill him! Kill him!* were now replaced with a scared, *What in the world have I done?* In the next hour or so, I stashed the gun with a friend and caught a bus for my grandmother's house on the west side of town. My grandmother's house had always been a place of refuge for me. I was a favorite of hers and was good at manipulating that. I told her I had done something crazy and needed to stay with her for a few days. In the end, she agreed. I was such a young, innocent, and baby-faced kid; I know she had no idea that I had just killed a man. At least at that point that's what I thought I had done. Once I emptied the gun, I just ran out of there as fast as I could.

Fortunately, however, I don't remember ever having shot a gun before that day, and five of the six bullets completely missed. The last one only caught him in the foot, but I didn't find that out until later. I believe that the grace of God was active in my life even then, and it protected me from killing him. Had any one of those bullets struck as I meant it to, I would probably still be in jail today.

After a few days at my grandmother's house, I returned to my home neighborhood. Again, I was stupid and drunk with my arrogance. I went right back to selling drugs and hanging out as I had before. The way I figured it, the gun was gone, there were no eyewitnesses, and I had gotten away with it. But it didn't take long for Tony's girlfriend or someone to call the police and say that I was the one who'd met Tony on the street that afternoon.

I was on one of our corners with the gang when the squad car pulled up. At first, I just thought they were coming to harass us like they did every now and then, but when they grabbed me and cuffed me, it was different. In our gang, it improved your rep to get arrested, so I was all cool like it was no big deal. I had to put on a show for the others and do the "this-ain't-nothing" walk to the squad car. I really had no idea what was happening until I got to the precinct and they booked me. Only then did I realize that life behind bars was no picnic.

They charged me with attempted murder as an adult. Luckily I didn't have any drugs on me when I was picked up, so there were no charges for dealing yet. My mom put up our house to get me out on bail while awaiting the trial. I was placed in her custody and given an eight o'clock curfew. But as soon as I was out of jail, I was back on the streets doing everything I had before. I would sneak back out after curfew to hang with my gang friends, deal drugs, and mess around with girls. If anything, I grew more brazen than ever, because now my rep was tougher than ever. Because I had shot a guy in our own gang, some were afraid of me and avoided getting in my way.

I was sure I would get away with it, too. The gun had never surfaced again. I was still so young and innocent looking that no one could believe I would ever do something like that. I even convinced my parents that I hadn't done it. A lot of the police in the area knew me because I used to work at a little pizzeria in the neighborhood, and they couldn't believe I would have shot anyone. The police never even searched my house. They probably figured that even if I did do it, even a stupid criminal would have gotten rid of the gun by then. There were no witnesses, so it was basically Tony's word against mine.

Around this time, I also got hooked up with a Jamaican gang. The gang members liked me and gave me big packages to sell for them. Because of what had happened with Tony, though, I was afraid to stash it where someone else might steal it, so I started carrying it around with me all of the time in a big shopping bag. I can't believe I was ever so stupid as to think that this would be safer, but I was. I was deceived in so many ways, and deception makes you really stupid.

So there I was, up on charges for attempted murder and walking the streets, standing on the corners, going everywhere I went with a grocery bag filled with enough marijuana and cocaine to put me away for decades. We knew there were patrol cars and undercover narcotics officers—"narcs," we called them—all over, but there I was anyway with my entire stash on me almost all of the time. I was totally messed up, but it would still get worse before it got better.

I did know enough to be jumpy, and that is what finally got me in trouble. I was standing on the corner with some of my friends, and two undercover policemen came up to talk with me and ask me some questions. If I had just stood there, I don't think anything would have made them pay much attention to me, but when I saw them coming, I thought I had been set up again, so I ran. The officers didn't chase me because they didn't even know who I was, but my running must have caused them to wonder about me and want to talk to me the next time they saw me. After that, they began keeping an eye out for me.

A couple of weeks later I was walking through the apartments again, and they saw me. This time they weren't going to let me go. As soon as I saw them, I bolted again, but this time they followed, and I couldn't outrun them. I was so dumb I didn't even dump my stash along the way, so when they finally caught me, my days of freedom on the streets were over for a while. Getting arrested this second time was much different from the first. This time I was terrified. I knew they had me because they had evidence this time, and after my first taste of being locked up, I had no desire to go back no matter what it did for my reputation. I knew as I rode to the precinct in the back of the car this time that my life would never be the same again.

Charges of possession of narcotics with intent to distribute were now added to my attempted murder charge, and I was sent to a maximum-security juvenile detention center to await trial. There would be no bail this time. As far as I was concerned, they had locked me away for good. The detention center was all cages and bars. Though we each had our own cells to sleep in, we spent most of our time revolving from the cafeteria, where we could watch TV, to the gym and recreation area. There were two groups of us that they always kept separate—one in one area and one in the other. When it was time to rotate, they would have us go down these hallways and into a caged area that was gated. When both groups were locked into these hallways, they would open the gates so we could exit into the other area so that there was never a chance the groups could get at each other.

Since I was up on charges for violent assault, I was in with the worst of the worst, but this time my baby-faced looks only brought me grief. This was the first place I had to really learn to fight on my own. In the hood, I had always had my gang to back me up, so most of the time others backed down, but here it was just me. Luckily guards were everywhere, and any scuffles got shut down quickly, because I don't think I would ever have held my own against any of these guys for long. I fought more in those two months than I have in all the other years of my life put together, but I also did everything I could to keep my nose clean. I wanted out.

The detention center was overcrowded, and because I did everything I could to stay out of trouble, they transferred me to a minimum-security facility after two months. I waited there another month before my trial. The difference between the two facilities was like night and day.

Fortunately again, my mother intervened by getting a good lawyer, and the charges were plea-bargained down to juvenile assault and distribution of drugs. I ended up spending roughly the next year in what was called *forestry camp*. One of the things I remember was what the judge said: "I'm sending you to forestry camp, but I really don't believe that they can help you. You are a menace to society." Had not God stepped in, I am sure he would have been right.

Forestry camp was out in the woods near Cumberland, Maryland, and we spent our days in three parts. In the morning we would cut trees and pick apples and peaches in an area where you wouldn't think fruit would grow, or do whatever odd jobs they could come up with for us. The camp would get part of the money, and we would get part of the money. The second part of the day we would be in school working to earn our GEDs. The evenings were spent in group counseling sessions. There were no bars or armed guards, and you could have walked off the property at any time, but you knew if you did, the next place they put you wouldn't be as open. So again I did what I could to fit into the system and stay out of trouble.

It was the job of the counselors to evaluate whether one of the detainees had reformed and was ready to be released. There was no set time for us to be there—we were just supposed to stay until it was determined we had reformed. I was such a gifted talker and conformer that within about three months I think I had my counselor convinced I had really changed, though I knew in my heart I hadn't. My parole officer, however, saw it differently, and because he had the final say, I stayed in the camp about another nine months.

In that time I really did change. I grew very health conscious, watching what I ate and working out with the other guys to the point of actually putting some meat on my skinny bones. By the time I was released, I even believed myself that I could reform. I had earned my GED and was ready to take my place as a contributor to society instead of a criminal.

I was nearly sixteen and a half by the time they released me. My mother was so scared of me that she wouldn't take me back home to live with her. She still believed in me—I remember she used to say, "Zach, you are better than all of this"—but she was still afraid she couldn't handle me, so I went to live with my father.

By this time, my father was living alone again because his second wife had left him. I tell you, we were certainly two crazy brothers living together. He went from work to the bar to bed to work to the bar to bed, and I had just gotten out of juvie. Because I was on probation, I had to get a job, so I started working as an electrician's apprentice. I was determined that I could make it in the world, but I didn't know how fragile my chances were because all of my changes had only been on the outside. Inside I was still the insecure, scared kid looking for approval and escape from a life without love or purpose.

I still remember the day my hopes crumbled. One day I missed the bus for work and had no way to get to my job at a construction site in Glen Burnie. It was an innocent mistake. It was mid-winter, cold, and the bus left before first light at 7:00 a.m. sharp. I was just moving a bit slower that day than usual and missed it by a few minutes. So rather than going home, I just hung out. I didn't do anything bad; I just walked the streets and enjoyed my freedom for the day. I didn't hook up with any of the old gang or even cruise the old neighborhood; I just took a day off.

The cruncher came that night when I got home. Unbeknownst to me, my dad had an agreement with the guy who had hired me that if there was any problem at all, he was to call my dad and let him know. So when I didn't show, he called. That night, instead of asking what had happened, my dad decided to try to trap me, so he asked, "How was work?"

When I answered, "Fine," he hit the roof.

Being a detective, I am sure he was ashamed of having a parolee for a son and was distrustful and suspicious by nature. I was guilty until proven innocent because of my one little lie. Add to that the drinking and the emotional extremes to which alcoholism can drive people, and when he exploded it was both physical and verbal. "You're still doing that stuff, aren't you?" he accused. "You went with your druggie friends again, weren't you? Don't lie to me again! You haven't changed! What am I going to have to do to get through to you?"

With each physical blow and verbal tirade, my hope for the future was crushed. All of the self-confidence and change I had put on in forestry camp lay as rubble in my heart. I thought, *Nothing I do will ever be good enough—so why try?* In that moment, I virtually gave up on life.

By that weekend, I had contacted some of my cousins who were still selling drugs and bought a bag to sniff in the basement that night. Before long I was using so much I had to sell as well to have enough money to supply my growing habit. With that I again felt the confidence and independence of having money in my pocket. It started with little deals, but it wasn't long before I was back into it full swing. Without some kind of outside help, I was headed back into trouble fast. That help wasn't going to come through either of my parents. Rock bottom wasn't far away.

The Slippery, Subtle Path to Destruction

When Tony didn't kill me in the street that evening and prison didn't hold me until I was old and gray, the devil didn't just give up and say, "Well, I guess this one is too tough; might as well let him succeed." No; instead, I locked even more deeply into the counterfeit identity I had found, and Plan C went into effect: I would waste the rest of my life away on drugs or simply overdose to cut it short.

From my time in forestry camp until I was about nineteen, I went from smoking marijuana to sniffing cocaine. By eighteen or so,

I was completely addicted, and my first thought every morning was not about what was for breakfast or about what I was going to do that day, but about where my next hit would come from. I was strung out 24/7, which meant I stayed high twenty-some hours a day and slept two or three, then rolled out of bed to take my next snort and start all over again. To get those few hours of sleep each night, I drank alcohol to counteract the high of the cocaine, which would relax me enough to finally let me doze off. It was a downward spiral, and any glamour or coolness I had seen as a twelve-year-old was gone. I was a total slave to my addiction.

Never Too Late

Key #3

The people you hang with become a prophecy of your future. Who is in your circle of influence?

✛

My son, do not walk in the way with them,
Keep your foot from their path;
For their feet run to evil,
And they make haste to shed blood....
They lie in wait for their own blood,
They lurk secretly for their own lives.

—Proverbs 1:15–16, 18

Many times when Christian leaders give testimonies of the crazy, wild times they had in their younger days with parties, alcohol, sex, drugs, and rock 'n' roll, they end their talks with: "And then I met Jesus, and now everything is better. So you should try Jesus, too." *The end.* Because so much of their testimony relates to the past, the appeal of those days in sin comes through as strongly as—if not stronger than—their call to be saved.

For me, I don't see it that way at all. Certainly there was something enjoyable in my years of partying, meeting girls, and having hundreds of dollars in my pocket. But the devastating pain and agonizing emptiness I felt in those years after forestry camp has blurred my memory of those younger, foolhardy years. No high I ever felt could even came close to compensating for the lows of those later years. My lows lasted months at a time and would have lasted years if they'd had the chance.

Only people who have experienced such addiction know the desperation that comes with it. It's as close to actually living in hell as I can imagine. Nothing satisfies but getting back to your drugs, and even that only takes the edge off of things for a short time. Not only that, but my body began falling apart. My nose would start bleeding unexpectedly, or I would blow it and pieces of cartilage would come out. I hardly ever ate, but lived off the calories from the alcohol I drank. I had lost almost all self-control.

Since my father was always at the bars, he was never around much, so I did whatever I wanted to do. By the time I was eighteen, my addictions were so severe that I couldn't sell enough drugs to keep myself supplied with what I used personally. For extra money, I got a job in the collections department of a fitness club. I only got the job because someone I sold drugs to worked there. Since I couldn't even make it an hour without my drugs, every chance I had I would sneak off to snort. On bathroom breaks, I would go into the stalls and sniff cocaine. At lunchtime I would sneak out to my car in the parking lot and duck down beneath the steering wheel to take another hit. I brought girls over to the house, got them high, and then slept with them. Looking back today I find it hard to believe that I survived, didn't totally destroy my liver or lungs, didn't contract AIDS, or didn't do some other permanent damage to my body.

Too many people try to deny that the devil exists. This is one of his greatest ploys—so he can take his time to destroy them or catch them unexpectedly. Far too many people live "whatever-will-happen-will-happen" lifestyles, thinking destiny is totally up to God. They fail to understand that the devil has a destiny for them as well and that he has created a whole world system of lies and traps to keep them from the destiny God wants for them.

Now, I am not big into any "the devil made me do it" attitude. In all those years, the devil never made my decisions for me. He didn't decide for me to start running and selling drugs. He didn't pull the trigger on that gun and unload six shots intending to kill Tony. He didn't light my first marijuana cigarette or lay out my lines of cocaine for me. And to be quite frank, he wasn't the one who invited women over to my house or unbuckled my belt for me when I was with them. All of that was me. I did those things of my own free, deceived, self-ish, stupid will. I'm sure there have been thousands who have done less and paid for it with their lives.

The world we live in is booby-trapped with a system of half-truths that counterfeit the desires of our hearts, so that when we look for the good things God put in the earth for us, all we find are the devil's snares instead. He will blind us to the truth so that we don't know any better than to get sucked into his traps. He whispers into our ears, playing on our weaknesses and pride, just as he did when he put the thought into my head to kill Tony. He takes the truths of desiring wealth, meaningful relationships, friendship and family, work and accomplishment God intended for our fulfillment in life and distorts them to make them lead to death instead. He circles us as much as he can in darkness so that we stumble again and again and can never find our way out.

And that's where I was—in the dark, making wrong decisions, trapped by my own choices. I had chosen the quick and dirty instead of the high and holy. What I needed was light and a healthy fear of God to snap me out of it.

Thank God, He sent me just that in the form of someone who cared enough to start praying for me with a heart just like Jesus'.

Three

God Never Gives Up on the Destiny He Put in You

And the Lord said, "Simon, Simon! Indeed, Satan has asked for you, that he may sift you as wheat. But I have prayed for you, that your faith should not fail; and when you have returned to Me, strengthen your brethren."

—*Luke 22:31–32*

I'T'S STRANGE TO think back and realize that it was a dream that saved my life.

I was definitely bottoming out, and I doubt I would have lived much longer had God not thrown me a lifeline. Even though I was making good money at the fitness center and still selling drugs, my addiction was outrunning my cash flow, so everything in my life was falling apart, including my car. It wasn't long before it finally completely broke down on me, and I didn't have the money to fix it. I then had a choice to make: I could either ride the bus home, which was hard on me because it was such a long time away from my drugs, or I could catch a ride with a guy named Douglas who just happened to work on the same floor of the fitness club as I did and only lived about ten houses down the street from me.

Douglas was the natural choice, except for one thing: I had been avoiding Douglas from the time I started working at the fitness center. Douglas was what we all called "one of those Jesus freaks" or "a Holy Roller," and I had been warned about him soon after I started at the fitness center. I did everything I could to avoid him.

What I didn't know was that shortly after I had started working there, Douglas had heard about me too, and when he found out I lived just up the street from him, he decided to start praying for me.

Now Doug has never been the type of guy to pray a sweet, little "Jesus, save him and bless him" prayer for anyone and leave it at that. Doug was—and still is—the type of guy for whom the words *prayer* and *passion* are connected at the hip. He never did one without feeling the other, or felt the one without doing the other. Doug walked the floor praying for me in his house as he did for anything else God put on his heart, and I am not sure he has ever stopped.

So when my car broke down and I had the choice of taking the bus or riding with Doug, I decided to risk riding with Doug, because the most important thing to me was getting home to my drugs as quickly as possible. I knew I had to ride with him, but I didn't want to talk with him, so I came up with a plan. I would ignore him, or whenever he asked me a question, I would just say *yes* really fast as if I had been listening the whole time. I figured that would make him happy, and I could keep riding with him until I got my car fixed or found a better solution. This time the devil's trap—my addiction to cocaine—led me right into God's trap—being in a car with a Jesus freak.

So when I got in his car that first day—I remember that it was a Tuesday—it wasn't two minutes before he started witnessing to me about Jesus. So I put my plan into action. I remember saying, *yes, yes, yes, yes, yes,* to everything he asked me. However, suddenly something he said caught my ear. He started talking about hell and describing what it was like. He told me about how hot it would be, and I remember thinking, *Man, that's not a place I want to go if it's going to be that hot.* At least I had the presence of mind to realize that I didn't want to go to hell, and I believe it was when that seed of truth sank into my heart that something happened.

That night I went through my usual routine of sniffing cocaine and then drinking until I could fall asleep for my handful of hours. But when I finally dozed off, I had a dream like none I'd ever had before.

In the dream I was in a small room the size of a gas station bathroom. It had only one door and no windows. At first it was just claustrophobic, but then these shadowy things began to appear and started floating around the room. They had no bodily shape or real form, but were black silky things that gave me a chill each time I looked at them. Before long they started circling me, and then they suddenly started flying at my head. I waved my arms to bat them away, but my hands had no effect on them. Soon I was doing everything I could to fight them off. I started running around the room, frantically swinging my arms and screaming. I tried the door, but it wouldn't open. I pounded on it and called for someone to help me, for someone to open the door and let me out. But after only a few seconds of this, I started waving my arms at the flying things again because I couldn't stand letting them come at me without fighting back somehow—even if it was useless. I couldn't do anything to make them stop or find any relief from their constant barrage. I was being completely overwhelmed, and I began to panic. It was more horrible than you can imagine.

Then, just when I thought I couldn't take it anymore, the door began to open slowly, and a bright light came in through the opening.

As it did, the things flying around my head seemed to take notice. For an instant they froze, hanging in the air as if suspended from the ceiling. When I got that moment of reprieve, I looked up to see who had opened the door. I saw Doug stick his head inside to see what was going on. The minute he did, the flying things fled.

At that, I awoke immediately, shaking and crying. For the next three nights, every time I shut my eyes, I had that same exact dream, every detail the same, every color the same, always the same room, the same silky black forms flying at me, and the same feelings of horror and complete and utter helplessness.

By the fourth night—which was the Friday of that week—I couldn't bring myself to sleep because I knew I would have that dream again. I was scared. I didn't want to go back to that little room and be at the mercy of those shapeless shadows ever again. I didn't want to wake up shaking and crying again. I was really in a bad position, because I hadn't been sleeping much up until then anyway, and now I was scared of ever going back to sleep again. I got high again, but it didn't help. I was so terrified I just wandered around my room, exhausted, but unwilling to lie down and get some rest. Then somehow, in my fear and delirium, I must have walked out of my house and down the street. All I remember is that I found myself at Doug's door, banging on it and crying for him to let me in and to help me.

Even though it was late, probably nearly midnight, Doug came to the door and opened it. The minute I saw him I simply said, "I'm ready."

Doug didn't need any further explanation. He let me in and walked me down the stairs to his basement, because that is where he did most of his praying. We knelt together, and I said a simple sinner's prayer that went something like this:

Jesus, I believe You are the Son of God, born of the virgin Mary, and that You died for my sins and rose for my victory.

From this moment forward, I renounce my allegiance to this world and pledge allegiance to the lordship of Jesus Christ in my life. I welcome the precious Holy Spirit into my heart to lead me and guide me into all truth. I ask for Your help to break free from every ungodly habit and addiction in order that I might walk out Your plan and destiny for my life from this moment forward. In Jesus' name, amen.

I don't think it even took four minutes, but when I got up, it was beyond all shadow of a doubt that something that happened. I was saved, and, in the twinkling of an eye, I'd been transformed.

Never Too Late

Key #4

The best setup is a God setup! Say *yes* when He makes an offer you can't refuse.

✠

How long, you simple ones, will you love simplicity?
For scorners delight in their scorning,
And fools hate knowledge.
Turn at my rebuke;
Surely I will pour out my spirit on you;
I will make my words known to you....
But whoever listens to me will dwell safely,
And will be secure, without fear of evil.

—PROVERBS 1:22–23, 33

Now when some people get saved, they say the prayer and don't feel anything, even though they are, in that exact moment, reborn just as I was. For me, it wasn't anything spectacular like seeing Jesus standing before me with His arms opened to me, or a bright light washing away the darkness in my life. But when I stood up from praying with Doug, I instantly knew all of my drug addiction had evaporated. I mean, when I got up, it was simply gone. My three years of addiction was so gone, in fact, that when I got home I flushed all the drugs I had left in the house down the toilet, and I never experienced any symptoms of withdrawal or any cravings for drugs ever again. In that instant, I was radically changed.

I was so excited about it that I had to tell someone, so I got on the phone in the middle of that same night and called my cousins to tell them. I wanted them to know there was a way out. "I'm done with drugs," I told them. "I'm finished with the selling; I'm finished with the using. I don't ever want to have anything to do with drugs again in my life!"

That was in April of 1989, roughly a month before my twentieth birthday, and I have never been tempted to use drugs again since that day.

That Sunday, two days later, I attended church with Doug at the Living Word Christian Center and stayed a loyal member there for the next seven years.

God Cares More About Your Future Than He Does About Your Past

Every day, people come to my church with problems like I had in my teen years in Baltimore, and my message to them has never changed. God doesn't make mistakes. He has never given up on you. God loves you and wants to see you fulfilled in life. God has a purpose and calling—a destiny—that He seeded into you when you were first conceived in your mother's womb, and He is still holding it for you today. When He looks at you, He sees your destiny fulfilled, not dead. Certainly, if you have wasted some years of your life, you may have to work overtime a bit to still accomplish it, but that doesn't bother God. He is still big enough to help you do it and willing to spend the effort on you to get it done.

When you are driving a car, have you ever noticed how big your windshield is compared to how big your rearview mirror is? Your rearview mirror is tiny compared to all the windows that are put in the car so that you can see out. Why is that? Because that is how much more important *where you are going* is than *where you have been*. Certainly we can look back and learn from the mistakes or triumphs we have had in the past, but we don't spend all our time looking in the rearview mirror. If we did, we would crash into whatever is just ahead of us. We only need to take a glimpse at what is behind us every once in a while to make sure it doesn't creep up on us unawares. The rest of the time we spend looking at where we are going, checking our dashboard to see how fast we are heading there, and checking the engine gauges and lights to make sure all is running smoothly. We make sure we have enough gas and that the air is the right temperature. We play the right kind of music on the radio.

Destiny is not about where we have been; it's about what we are doing now in the present to make sure we are headed where God wants us to go in the future. That is the place we want to be. That is where we will find our ultimate life's fulfillment. That is the race we discipline ourselves to run so that we will never be disqualified from all God wants us to be and to have.

More than any other Bible writer, the apostle Paul seemed to understand this. Look at what he said in his letter to the Philippians:

> This one thing I do, forgetting those things which are behind, and reaching forth unto those things which are before, I press

toward the mark for the prize of the high calling of God in Christ Jesus.

—PHILIPPIANS 3:13–14, KJV

In order to get the full weight of this passage of Scripture, it is important to realize who Paul was when he said these words. Paul had been an incredible success in his world. He came from the right family and lived only in the best neighborhoods. He'd graduated from all of the right schools, studied under the Nobel laureates of his time, been the president of his fraternity, and, in effect, gone straight from college to being partner in one of the largest law offices of his day. If there was success to be had in the Jewish world of Paul's day, he had experienced it, yet when he talks of this, he says, pretty bluntly:

I count all things but loss for the excellency of the knowledge of Christ Jesus my Lord: for whom I have suffered the loss of all things, and do count them but dung, that I may win Christ.

—PHILIPPIANS 3:8, KJV

That's right; he calls all the things he accomplished as a loss rather than a gain compared to knowing Jesus, or, as he says with more emphasis, all those things were "dung"—that's right, *manure*—compared to accomplishing what God had called him to do in his life. That is a pretty bold statement and completely the opposite of the way most people in the world would see it.

But that is not all that Paul was. He may have accomplished great things, but he had also done horrible, unspeakable things. Paul had been a first-century terrorist. He had imprisoned, kidnapped, bound, and murdered men, women, and children because of his legalistic religious beliefs. While Stephen was being stoned to death, he stood by holding the coats of the men murdering Stephen so that the coats wouldn't get dirty or splattered by Stephen's blood. He traveled his world like a bounty hunter to find Christians and bring them with their hands tied back to Jerusalem to be judged and sentenced by the high religious council. And he thought he was doing it all to the glory of God! It wasn't until he met Jesus face-to-face on the road to Damascus that he realized that the one true God doesn't do things that way. He is a God of love, not of punishment and execution.

So Paul knew he had to forget and leave behind these horrifying acts, too. They were all forgiven by Jesus' sacrifice on the cross, and he was washed clean by the blood of the lamb. His past sins were tossed in the sea of forgetfulness with a *No Fishing* sign posted over it. Paul had both accomplished more worldly honors and done more ghastly things than most of us have even imagined, yet he said that he would put them all behind him for the hope of accomplishing what God had set before him. We need to do the same thing.

Realize that wherever you are today, God still believes in you. He also still believes in the loved ones you may be concerned about and are praying for, even if they don't believe in Him. It's never too late. If you need to turn your life around, then you can pray just as I did, and your change will start today. If you have a loved one who needs that kind of change, than you need to be that person's Douglas and start passionately praying for God's light and changing truth to come into their lives. God's destiny is still there to be realized, buried as a seed in our hearts. Now that you know it is there, you need to learn how to take the next step of nurturing it into life and reaching forth for the prize of the high calling God has for each of us in Jesus!

Part Two

Nurture the Seed
of Your Destiny

Four

Find an Identity That Matches Your Destiny
(You Can't Do It Alone)

As iron sharpens iron,
So a man sharpens the countenance of his
friend.

—Proverbs 27:17

OR THE NEXT seven years, every time the doors of the Living Word Christian Center were open for services, and I wasn't working or sick or something like that, I was there. Even when I was working late on Wednesday nights, I would come straight from work to the services even though it meant coming late. I was so hungry for all God had to offer me that you couldn't keep me away. Almost immediately I also started attending the Maranatha Bible School, which was part of Living Word's outreach programs, and as I began to spend more time in the Word, I began to hear the direction of God in my heart.

For me, being saved was like flipping on a light switch inside of me that I had been ignoring for nineteen years. I know it is not like that for everyone, but for me I went from wanting only to satisfy my own desires twenty-four hours a day to wanting to please God with my every action. Yet it is one thing to want something, and quite another to do it. I had changed dramatically on the inside, but it would take years for that to show up on the outside.

For one thing, while my addiction to cocaine disappeared overnight, other habits I had formed in my teens did not. First of all, I was still bound to cigarettes. After that night at Doug's house and the change it wrought in my life, the idea of putting anything impure into my body became repulsive to me. However, my body was still hooked on nicotine, and from March of 1989 when I was saved until August of that year, I really struggled against lighting up. In my heart, I didn't want to smoke anymore, but there I would be, still smoking regularly, but doing it with tears streaming down my face because I wanted to stop so badly. I would get so angry about it I would throw my last pack of cigarettes out the window on the way home, only to rush back out soon after to buy another carton.

Another problem I had was with promiscuity. This, oddly enough, was even one step further out than cigarettes had been. I had been delivered of my worst addiction when I got saved. Although I was not delivered of cigarettes, I immediately knew in my heart of hearts that it was wrong. However, I had no such immediate crisis of conscience with my relationships with women. It was something I wasn't willing to submit to right away.

Now I wasn't "sleeping around" recklessly, but I did always have a girlfriend whom I could be with. I was so naïve to the ways of God that I had no idea there was anything wrong with exercising my sexuality outside of marriage, until one day I bragged to Doug about a new girlfriend I had recently been with and he set me straight. Even then I didn't fully agree with him. I was attending church by then and tried to justify my philandering with Scripture. When I read the passage in 1 Corinthians 7 that states, "It is better to marry than to burn with passion," I thought to myself, *Yeah, why burn? I don't need that! It is healthier to let it go and release my passions than to keep it all bottled up inside!* (See 1 Corinthians 7:9.) Of course, in doing so, I was perverting what the scripture was really saying and making it fit my life the way I wanted it to fit. However, this resistance to God's truth didn't last long, and I soon had to acknowledge what the Word really said and change accordingly.

I have seen people go years continuing to live in promiscuous lifestyles without ever really changing. Looking back at this time of my life, I recognize why I was able to become obedient to sexual purity in only a handful of months. I don't attribute that to anything special about me, but to the discipling I received from Doug. He took it upon himself to teach me how to pray as he did, and, as a result, every night I was brought before the throne of God. Because of continuous exposure to that kind of light, I grew more and more sensitive to the Word and to what the Holy Spirit was trying to do in my life.

Doug was a man of habit, and he taught me to be the same. With my new lifestyle, I didn't fit in so well at my dad's house anymore. In fact, he seemed to think I had joined some wacky group of fanatics, because suddenly all I would talk about was the Bible and what it said. In addition, Doug had counseled me to stay clear of the people I used to hang out with until I was stronger in my faith, especially my cousins. So, I ended up over at Doug's house almost every night of the week—especially on weekends—often eating dinner with him and his wife and the choir director from the church. At work, we always ate lunch together. In fact, it wasn't long until I was transferred to his unit at the fitness center, and we started working together until he left to be an associate pastor at the church.

For those first few years, it seemed like everywhere Doug went, I was there, too. Because he was a key leader in the church, I got to know everyone there very quickly. He was popular, so I soon became popular also through hanging out with him. Suddenly I had gone from the unhealthy environment of the streets to hanging out with people who were going places. It was quite a transition, and I had found a new group to fit in with who weren't trying to take anything away from me, but who were to be a blessing to me instead.

The thing is, though, that every night after dinner, Doug would go to his basement to pray, and I don't mean a little five-minute prayer, either. Doug would pray until he had heard from heaven—until he was in the Spirit and could hear what God was trying to say to him. His prayer time didn't have an ending time specified; he just prayed until he felt released from praying for the night. Some nights I would enter in too, but other nights I would pray that God would hurry up and speak to him so that we could finish for the evening. But all that time spent in that basement seeking God in prayer began to slowly change me from the inside out. God was laying foundations in me that would not only transform me and deliver me from the other addictions of my life, but would also develop in me an ear for God's voice, which has proven crucial to where I am today as a pastor.

How Deliverance Comes

At the time, I really wondered why God didn't just deliver me of all my problems at once. But in the years since then, I have realized that God brings deliverance in different ways according to what is best for us. Sometimes it comes suddenly and sovereignly. God just reaches down into a person's life and touches that person. He may show His love and miracle-working power as a sign to someone of His existence or to relieve someone from a problem they can't solve without His intervention. He may act in power to answer someone's prayer, or for any number of reasons that God alone knows. This can happen to someone who is unsaved just as easily to someone who is saved. For His own reasons and without needing to explain it to us, God just reaches into our world and heals something. This is what He did in my life when I prayed that simple prayer that night, and if He sees fit, He can do the same in your life, too.

However, hoping for such a miracle can be fruitless. If God decides to move in that way, great. But even if He doesn't, He never leaves us without hope. This is what happened to me with cigarettes. It was a physical addiction I wanted to kick with all of my heart, but I had no strength to do it in my own will. So, for five months I sat in church under the leadership of the pastor, elders, and other men of God who ministered the Word to me every chance they got. As I learned to pray, study, and live the Word, and as I worshiped God with my whole heart, gradually I changed on the inside to such an extent that at the end of that time I could finally set that pack of cigarettes down and not pick them up again. Through my discipline in the Word and prayer, I had formed new spiritual strength inside of me that gave me the self-control to beat nicotine—my spirit had become strong enough to overrule my physical desires. It was just as miraculous as what had happened to me with drugs, but it took longer to come because there were things I had to do and to believe to be changed. Yet when I finally did set them down, I had kicked them just as much as I had kicked drugs out of my life.

> ## Never Too Late
>
> ## Key #5
>
> In life, you have two choices, *right* or *wrong*—there's not much left in the middle, and eventually you will have to choose.
>
> ☩
>
> I call heaven and earth as witnesses today against you, that I have set before you life and death, blessing and cursing; therefore choose life, that both you and your descendants may live.
>
> —DEUTERONOMY 30:19

You see, sin doesn't give God any trouble. It is not that He tolerates it, but when we turn to Him, if we are just lost sinners who didn't know how to live any better before we accepted Jesus as Lord and Savior, it is easy for Him to set us straight again. When sinners come to Jesus, it is easy for them to set aside their old lives to take on a new one in Christ, because it is so easy to see that what they had before was *only emptiness,* and what they have now is *fullness of life.* This is why Jesus had no problem converting and healing the masses of rough sailors and fishermen, prostitutes, and corrupt public officials. What He had to offer was obviously so much better that it was easy for them to desert their old ways for His new ways. And with that transformation of heart often came a healing transformation of the body as well. As Paul said:

> Therefore, if anyone is in Christ, he is a new creation; old things have passed away; behold, all things have become new.
>
> —2 CORINTHIANS 5:17

However, when God comes to perverted religious thinking that is based in selfish desire, that selfish mind-set has to be changed before He can bring this kind of transformation into that person's life. Jesus paid for every sin on the cross, but if we don't believe in that sacrifice and accept it, then it will not do us any good. Religious thinking is really just a form of unbelief—it is rejecting God's truths for our own, or, to put it another way, it is *not believing* what God says so that we can remain selfish and live the way we want instead of the way He has prescribed. While religious people may look good on the outside—like the most upstanding citizens in their communities—religion corrupts on the inside like a cancer of the soul.

This is why so few of the Jewish religious leaders Jesus addressed ever followed His teachings. Jesus often spoke to them harshly, trying to rattle them out of their conceited mind-sets and corrupt lifestyles. They were happier to live in their man-made traditions than in the truth. Look at what He said about them:

> All their works they do to be seen by men.... They love the best places at feasts, the best seats in the synagogues, greetings in the marketplaces, and to be called by men, "Rabbi, Rabbi" ["Teacher, Teacher"].... Woe to you, scribes and Pharisees, hypocrites! For you cleanse the outside of the cup and dish [you look righteous and good on the outside], but inside they are full of extortion and self-indulgence. Blind Pharisee, first cleanse the inside of the cup and dish [your hearts], that the outside of them may be clean also. Woe to you, scribes and Pharisees, hypocrites! For you are like whitewashed tombs which indeed appear beautiful outwardly, but inside are full of dead men's bones and all uncleanness. Even so you also outwardly appear righteous to men, but inside you are full of hypocrisy and lawlessness.
>
> —MATTHEW 23:5–7, 25–28

This is what my attitude toward sexual promiscuity was like when I first got saved. Rather than conforming immediately to what I saw in the Word of God about the matter, I tried to change what Scripture really said to fit my own selfish desires. Because of this, it took me even longer to kick that habit than it did to kick cigarettes. But I stayed in church under godly leadership and was hungry for the truth of the Word. Eventually the uncleanness of my sexual promiscuity was revealed for what it really was: sin that separated me from the full life God had for me, as well as hurting others who need real love, too.

In many ways these physical sins were easier to fix than spiritual ones. I am not saying one sin is better than another—they all lead to destruction—but physical sins such as smoking, promiscuity, or committing crimes are easily seen, and the self-righteous take great pride in condemning them while ignoring their own sins of injustice and favoritism, lack of mercy, arrogance, and unfaithfulness. We can never ignore one part of the Word and condemn another. This is the very definition of being a hypocrite. What we must instead do is remain steady in applying the Word to all parts of our lives, letting it transform us and give us new and healthier mind-sets.

Jesus Called Us to Be Disciples, Not Just Converts

Far too many in churches today are happy to become converts to Christianity and then just sit in the pew and ride life out looking to eternity. If Jesus had come to the earth just to provide us a way to go to heaven, pew sitting would be fine. But the truth is, He didn't just save us for *us*. He saved us so that we would spread His kingdom across the entire earth.

What is His kingdom? Righteousness, peace, and joy in His Holy Spirit (Rom. 14:17). In other words, wherever these three things exist because a Christian has brought them there in the power of the Holy Spirit, God's love and judgments will be there as well. That will be a place where God is on the throne, and in God's love and judgments is everything we need to live life to its fullest.

Jesus needs people who are not content just to be *converts*—but those who desire to be *disciples*. At its essence, *disciple* is just a fancy word for *student*, and students need teachers. If you really want the fullness of life Jesus promises, then you need to be a student to teachers whom you see living the life you want to live. You need to find someone with a godly identity that enables your destiny, and you need to become a disciple to that person.

First and foremost, this means being a disciple of Jesus. You need to get to know Him through the Gospels and the rest of the Word, through spending time in prayer communicating with Him, and worshiping Him in your quiet times, with your church fellowship, and with your lifestyle.

Yet this is not enough. You also need the fellowship of other believers, both those who are going through the same experiences that you are and those who are more experienced in the things of God and can mentor and disciple you in how to live. It is peculiar to notice that most churches today don't have a formal process for discipling new believers. People come into churches, get saved, and then maybe attend some kind of membership class—and that's it. After that they are on their own.

I was blessed because I was discipled by Doug. When he prayed with me in his basement, he didn't just mark me down as a notch on his salvation list and go on to the next. He stayed with me, made sure I got plugged into the church he attended, met and prayed with me, and watched over me as I grew in the Lord. If I had questions, he was there to answer them. He was a man of God with whom I could identify, and he helped me grow into the destiny to which God had called me.

If you look at the biblical pattern, you will see that some of the most important leaders of God's people were discipled by godly men and women who functioned as their teachers. Joshua had Moses, David had Samuel, Elisha had Elijah, the disciples had Jesus, Paul had Barnabas, Mark had Barnabas and Peter, and Timothy had Paul, just to name a few. All of these men had other men to act as their teachers and mentors. Do we really think we can get away with any less today?

Outside of the typical Sunday school or Bible study format, discipleship and mentoring in the church seems to be a lost art today. This is probably true for a combination of reasons: many young people do not think they need to be mentored, and older believers are often too busy with their own lives to make mentoring new believers a priority. It is the essence of the generation gap. Regardless of the reasons, however, I believe this lack of discipling is really part of the world system's plan to keep Christians divided and powerless. If every believer is isolated from relationship with other believers and can learn only from the pastor's sermons, what real contact or community exists between the various parts of the church? Without any depth of relationship, it is no wonder that we—who are Jesus' body on the earth today—are so divided and powerless.

God has a different plan for His body. He thinks that His body on earth should operate *together*, like this:

> We should no longer be children…but, speaking the truth in love, may grow up in all things into Him who is the head—Christ—from whom the whole body, joined and knit together by what every joint supplies, according to the effective working by which every part does its share, causes growth of the body for the edifying of itself in love.
>
> —EPHESIANS 4:14–16

Young men and women, if you want to live in all that God has for you, then you need to be willing to listen to those who have been where you want to go. This could mean seeking out a businessman in your church and community from whom you can learn, or a husband and wife whom you see as great parents so they can help you as you raise your kids. It might mean finding the prayer warriors of your church and kneeling with them once a week to make intercession for others. It might mean standing next to the craziest worshiper you can find and trying to understand the joy that person has dancing before the Lord.

Fathers and mothers in Christ, you need to be willing to be open to sharing your experiences, good and bad, and your struggles in following the Lord so that others can learn from your triumphs and mistakes. You need to let others see your heart for God; open yourself up to let your wisdom season the zeal of those who are newer believers around you. Let them refire your passion for Christ even as you temper the things in their lives from which God needs to transform and deliver them.

We must never forget that coming to Jesus is just the first step in coming into our destinies. It is a process we must never stop until it is completely fulfilled. We are called to be His body on the earth, and we simply can't succeed without the help of others.

Jesus Calls Us Out From the World

Not only must you be in relationship with other believers, but it will also be necessary for you to change your environment and move away from those with whom you used to hang out. You can't live with the sin that always trapped you before and think you can stay clear of it. You can't keep the drugs around and think you will never use them.

If you want to save sex until you are married, you better not be taking members of the opposite sex back to your bedroom and closing the door. Once that fire of sexual passion is ignited, it is too hard to put out! If you want to be delivered of the world that is dragging you to hell, then you better not hang out in it any more!

If you are going to succeed in living your destiny, you have to separate from those who will try to pull you back into your past weaknesses.

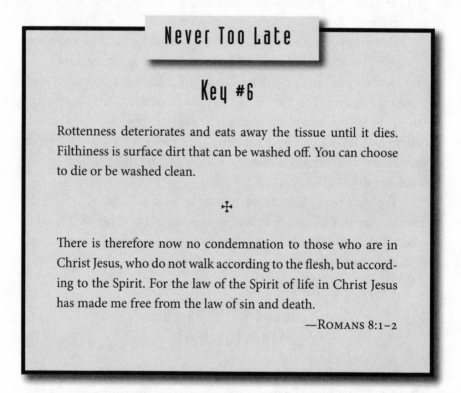

Never Too Late

Key #6

Rottenness deteriorates and eats away the tissue until it dies. Filthiness is surface dirt that can be washed off. You can choose to die or be washed clean.

✝

There is therefore now no condemnation to those who are in Christ Jesus, who do not walk according to the flesh, but according to the Spirit. For the law of the Spirit of life in Christ Jesus has made me free from the law of sin and death.

—ROMANS 8:1–2

Now I know you want to save the world, but if you just got delivered from marijuana, you don't need to go to a house that is full of marijuana. I am not saying you won't ever be able to walk in there, but not now, and especially not alone. When I first got saved, I did go back to the street corners and witness to some of the guys I had done drugs with, but I always did it with Doug or an evangelism team from our church.

1. When you first get saved, your first priority is to plant yourself in a good church and start to grow.

You have to get stronger in your new faith, you have to be discipled, and you have to get yourself built up in the Word of God until the truth of the Word replaces the lies you lived on the streets. Then maybe—just *maybe*—you can walk up to your old friends again and try to share Jesus with them. And that is a definite *maybe*. Too many get saved one day and then the next day go and try to save everyone with whom they were doing drugs, but instead of saving the others, they end up losing themselves. They get pulled right back into the sin. Then they feel condemned because they stumbled, and they don't want to go back to church because they feel like such failures. So one of the first things you have to do is separate from those who are operating in the same weaknesses that you used to operate in, because if you keep trying to hang out with them, all that will do is pull you back into those same weaknesses.

For example, I don't understand why one married woman would hang out with five single women, or why one married man would hang out with five single men. Once you get married, your priorities change. Single people spend a lot of time looking for members of the opposite sex to date, and they talk about them most of the time. They are still looking—but if you are married, you had better have stopped looking! If a person is single, they are available, looking for a spouse, but married folks aren't. If you are single, for the most part you are only responsible to yourself. You can hang out late, watch the Monday night game with friends, and go home whenever you would like. If you are married, you better be careful about doing that! You are no longer responsible just for yourself. You are responsible to your spouse as well, and don't be surprised if your spouse would rather have you hanging out with him or her than with your old single friends. Your priorities and responsibilities are different now, and you had better live accordingly.

2. It is also important that you get rid of all the memorabilia that reminds you of your old life.

This is very important. Some of you have large pictures on the walls of your house showing you with those gold teeth and big bush and a cigarette and a beer can. If you are looking at those reminders of your old life, you are just asking for trouble to come back into your life. Burn that picture, man! That was when you were Peewee; you're Mr. Reynolds now. That was when you were Náná, but you are Miss Johnson now. Back then you didn't know any better, but now you do. You don't need reminders of a past you want to leave in the past! You can't drive a car forward by looking backward all the time. If you try, you will crash! Even though the average driver travels twelve thousand miles a year moving forward for every one mile in reverse, more accidents happen while backing up than while going forward. Keep your eyes focused on where you are going!

You have got to get rid of that old memorabilia. If you're married now to Betty and you still have pictures of Sheila, then you are setting yourself up for trouble! Why do you still have pictures of Sheila in that box in the attic? Why are you up there looking at them? You are going to have some problems if your wife finds that box!

If you are going to leave all that behind, you definitely don't need to be reminded of how stupid you used to be. Dump that stuff and move on.

3. Look for those who are already positioned where you desire to be.

If I shouldn't hang around the people who are operating in the weaknesses that I have, then what should I do? I look for those who are already located where I want to be, people who have the strengths I would like to have. I was blessed to have an immediate example of what a Christian should be in Doug. I had a great mentor to disciple me. But I don't just mean this in being a Christian. If you feel a call to be in business, then try to hang out with business owners. If you want to grow up to be a doctor, see if you can't spend some time with a doctor. If you want to learn to be a leader in your church and community, make friends with other leaders and learn what they know.

Some people you would like to hang out with are beyond you, however. You might want to hang out with T. D. Jakes, Donald Trump, or John Maxwell, but you don't really run in those circles. Obviously you can't go everywhere, and neither can I. If some of the people you want to be like are inaccessible to you, then read their books or the books of people like them. If you can't afford to buy their books, you can check them out at the library, or if you don't have time to read, then you can check out their audio books. If they have lectures or sermons on tape or CD, you can listen to those—and don't just listen to them one time. Listen to them over and over to let the words get down into your heart and change the way you think.

Look for someone who is where you want to be and learn from his or her example.

4. Know how to keep on going when others stop.

Have you ever looked at a stepladder? At the top of the ladder, it says, "Do not sit or stand." Do you know why? Because it is dangerous to stay and get comfortable there while also reaching for something higher up. If you do, you are liable to tip it over and fall. So if you want to go up higher, the answer is simple: you need a bigger ladder.

The same is true in life. You can't afford to get comfortable and sit with those who aren't continually trying to grow. Doing that can cost you your destiny. If you find a ladder in life, climb to the top of it, and then think you can just sit there and wait for eternity, you are in trouble. *Destinies are not found in comfort zones.* You have to keep following God, and that may mean leaving everything behind as Abraham did. As destiny-minded Christians, we don't want to be following the crowd, but we want to be following the *cloud*—the glory cloud of God. We want to go where God wants us to go. As long as you are still living on this earth, God isn't finished with you yet. He is still expecting you to grow.

Faith doesn't live behind you; faith lives in front of you.

Look forward, and move forward. If there are opportunities to grow, take them. For the rest of eternity, God will always have more before us than behind us, but if we are always looking back, we will miss it. Don't stop climbing.

Five

The Treasure Within

For it is the God who commanded light to
shine out of darkness, who has shone in our
hearts to give the light of the knowledge of
the glory of God in the face of Jesus Christ.
But we have this treasure in earthen vessels,
that the excellence of the power may be of
God and not of us.

—2 Corinthians 4:6–7

MY LIFE BEGAN to change quickly during the first summer I
was saved. Though I was still struggling with the physical
issues of continued addiction to cigarettes and changing
my thinking concerning exercising my sexuality, there were some
things that didn't change. Perhaps the strangest one had to do with

my desires to be successful as a businessman and feeling that I should have a good lifestyle because of it.

Of course, when I quit using drugs, I also quit selling. This had an immediate effect on my cash flow. Where I should have gotten ahead because of not needing to supply my addictions anymore, I was still falling behind because I no longer had the income from hustling. Once you are used to living with a certain level of income, it is difficult to adjust yourself back down again. When I had been selling drugs, it was part of the game to keep up the look, which meant new clothes all the time—new shoes about every week or so, new pro team gear as it became available, and always having a crisp new pair of designer jeans and gold ropes of jewelry around my neck. I had always looked the part and had fallen into a vanity that was nothing more than a worship of imagery and possessions.

The look almost cost me my life one time, though I still stuck to it. When I was just back on the street after coming out of forestry camp, someone had held me up for my drugs. After I had handed those over, he asked me for the gold ropes around my neck. I was so crazy, I didn't want to give them to him, so when someone walked by down the street—we were in an alley—I made a break for it. He leveled his gun right at me and fired—and I remember it being a very big gun, the kind we used to call "Smith and Wesson." But just before he fired, I hit an icy spot and went sprawling. Had I not fallen, I am not sure I would be alive today. Satan had taken another shot at me, and again God had saved me before I even knew Him. His mercy is a wonderful thing.

My problem was that I was so used to that lifestyle and having all that money, it was hard to turn my back on it and live from paycheck to paycheck. I had the strangest of all temptations—not to go back to using drugs, but to go back to selling them. I still had my job at the fitness club, was working in Doug's department there, and was doing well with it, but it just wasn't enough to keep up with my desire for everything I felt I wanted in life.

When I prayed about this, however, God never told me I was evil for wanting to have more or to do well in business. Instead, as I started to better learn how to follow Him, and as my prayer life deepened while I prayed alongside Doug in his basement night after night, the first thing I really felt God speak directly to my heart was that I should enroll in college. At first I wasn't really sure it was God, but I couldn't shake it off. I knew I had no way to pay for any classes and really had no idea what good going back to school would do me, but as I continued to pray about it, the desire just got stronger.

So sometime around July or August of 1989, just a few months after being saved and right before the fall term was to start, I prayed, "Well, Lord, if You want me to go to school, then here is what I am going to do. I will fill out an application for Towson State University to take classes part time. Now I don't have any SAT scores for them to look at, because I never took the SATs because I was in forestry camp. I have a GED and not a high school diploma, and I don't have any money for tuition even if they do let me in. But since I feel this is what You want me to do, I will do it. If it is really what You want, You will have to take care of the rest."

So I filled out the application and turned it in—and to my surprise, they accepted me.

My second dilemma was to figure out how to pay for it. In trying to figure this out, I talked with my grandmother to see what advice she might have. When I did, she replied, "Zach, I will tell you what. I will put your first semester on my credit card, because I think you need to do this. But if you are serious, you are going to have to figure out how to pay for the rest on your own."

I was floored. I was going to start attending college in just a few short days!

Now I came to my third dilemma: What was I supposed to take

for classes? Although I was becoming more convinced that God had indeed told me to go to college, He had given me no clues as to what He wanted me to take. It was the weirdest thing. He told me to go, but He was leaving the direction of it up to me!

So, my first semester I decided to take two general classes—sociology and psychology, which would count toward whatever major I ended up pursuing and would give me some time to think about my major. Looking back at it now, my thinking process on this was pretty funny. My first thought was to study to be a pharmacist. That's right; my first thought was that I should sell drugs again, only this time legally! However, as I looked into it, I saw how much chemistry and how many lab classes were needed to major in pharmacy, and I began to realize that this really wasn't my thing at all. It was too much work in subjects I wasn't really good at and didn't even like.

So I began to doubt whether I had really heard from God again. I mean, why would He send me to college and not tell me why? Plus I didn't even know how I would pay for the second semester. Was I just crazy and had missed it?

But again, the desire to stay in school didn't go away. So I kept rolling it around in my mind and praying about it. God stayed silent on the issue, but after a while, out of my own logic came the thought, *Hey, I have always been good with money; why don't I look into doing something with that?* I began to look through the catalog again, this time at business and accounting majors. This time the courses and the desires of my heart really seemed to fit, so I decided to major in accounting. God didn't need to tell me what to do; I just needed to plug into the destiny inside of me.

Around this time I began to find out about financial aid programs that were available to me, so I filled out the paperwork for what was called a Pell grant. Again to my amazement, I was accepted to receive enough money from Pell grants to pay for my next four and a half years of school! In all I would attend university for five and a half years because I wasn't taking a full load every term, but in that time, my grandmother paid for the first semester, the Pell grants paid for the next four and a half, and by the time I was ready to graduate, I had enough money to pay for my last semester!

So, since the fitness collections office made calls from 9:00 a.m. to 9:00 p.m., I found I could still work thirty to forty hours a week and take a full load at the university at the same time. As a result, those were some pretty busy years. For a while there, I was attending Bible college at Living Word, going to services whenever I could, working at the fitness center, and working on my accounting degree at the university. With this radical new schedule, my life began to change quickly.

One of the first changes was in the way I did my job at the fitness center. As a collections department, it was our job to call people who were late in paying their bills to try to get them to pay. Part of our salary was a commission of how much we recouped for the company. In my first years at this job, I was merciless, partly because I was unsaved, but also partly because I was always high while doing it. I would badger people for not paying their health spa bills. I was very aggressive and threatened to destroy people's credit histories if they didn't pay up immediately. After I was saved, I became much more civil, but I also had incredible favor. I found I was still doing very well at getting people to pay despite my change in manner and tactics. I found I had a gift for explaining situations to people so that they could understand it and to persuade them to pay what they owed.

I also moved back in with my mother around this time. She was living alone, and I felt I should have been living with her rather than my father. I began seeing a lot of the guys I used to sell drugs with on the corner where I had first started. By this time, though, I was so changed and so on fire for God, there was no risk of me falling back into their lifestyle. Instead, I started pulling them into mine—I started leading them to the Lord left and right. Doug and I would often go out and hang with the gang members and drug salesmen on the corners and tell them about Jesus and the new life He offered to them. We led several of the guys I had done drugs with and sold drugs with to the Lord. I soon got a reputation for this at our church. Somebody gave me the nickname, "Zach, Zach, the Holy Ghost Maniac." It wasn't long before my mother came to the Lord as well.

All these results in evangelizing the people I knew were because of this crazy kind of fire that was burning in my heart. I spent hours in the basement—the same one where I used to stash my drugs—walking the floor and praying for that neighborhood. I can remember my mother yelling down the stairs because I was praying so loud it was coming up through the vents! You see, I had learned to pray from Doug, and with my fervency and passion came a good deal of volume. Yet as I prayed it also opened myself up for God to work on me and change me. I think whatever mental damage had been done by my drug abuse was healed during those hours of walking the floor of that basement pleading before the throne of God. I was developing my mind as I never had before, filling it with the Word, letting it soak in the presence of the Holy Spirit, and filling it with new knowledge at the university.

Don't let me fool you, though; the hood was still the hood, and it had grown even rougher in the decade between when I was a kid there and when I came back as Zach, Zach, the Holy Ghost Maniac. In my time of witnessing I was held up, shot at, and even, oddly enough, shot in the foot. I was with a team witnessing in a hard-core Jamaican section of town when a drug dealer, trying to clear the corner to say that it was his turf, shot at the ground to scare us off, but one of the bullets hit me instead. The bullet passed cleanly between my Achilles' tendon and my anklebone. Had it been a fraction of an inch in either direction, I might never have walked or done anything athletic again. It was so clean, in fact, I didn't even know I had been hit until we stopped running about a mile down the street and I realized I was bleeding.

Three of the first questions I ask Jesus when I get to heaven will be:

1. When I unloaded that gun at Tony that night, why did I only hit him in the foot?

2. Why didn't I get delivered of my addiction to cigarettes at the same time that God delivered me from cocaine?

3. Did my having shot Tony in the foot have anything to do with me getting shot in the foot just a few years later?

Taking Hold of Your Destiny

As I look back at those early years of faith, I see God's fingerprints everywhere working to fulfill His blueprint for my life. Yet despite His desires for our good, He has also given us free will, meaning He will never overpower our wills to enforce His will upon us. Though He always knows what's best for us and must constantly be hurt by our hurting ourselves, the only way His will can be realized in our lives is if we want it and pursue it. He is more than willing to come 95 percent of the way to us if we are willing to go 5 percent of the way in pursuing Him.

In those years, I have also identified some keys to finding our destinies that I think are important for all of us to realize.

1. Finding our destiny is a matter of pursuing intimacy with God with all of our hearts.

Now, I am not talking about religion. Religion tends to give you lists of things—dos and don'ts, what God is like, how to please Him, explanations of the way the world works, and so forth. These things aren't necessarily bad in and of themselves, but they really cause you to miss the point of what being a Christian is all about. If you got married, would you want to be with your wife most of the time, or would you be content to sit with your sister-in-law and let her tell you stories about what your wife is like, what she did as a kid, what she told her the last time they spoke, what pleases her, and what makes her angry? You would want to be with your wife, of course! Does that mean that sitting with your sister-in-law and learning about your wife is bad? Of course not, but if that is all you ever did, I wouldn't have much hope for your marriage!

The same is true with God. If we spend all of our time listening to what other people know of God and never spend any time with Him ourselves, do we have much hope of ever really hearing from Him for ourselves? Yet despite this, millions of Christians are content to go to church every Sunday and just sit in church to hear their pastors' or priests' thoughts on God, what He has told them lately, what they learned about Him in seminary, and what they think pleases Him. They never take any time to pursue God and know Him for themselves. This often happens because they have been raised in religion, which tells them they are not holy enough to know God unless they are like their pastors or priests. So they believe that the best they can do is to sit and listen to their spiritual leaders because the ministers know, and those in the pews do not.

If there was one good thing that came from me growing up as a drug dealer, it was that I learned that religion (instead of relationship with God) is empty. Even though I'd attended church only a few times growing up, I knew people who went to church on Sunday and then lived the same drug-infested lifestyle I lived the rest of the week. Church didn't seem to do anything for them. By the time I got up off of my knees in Doug's basement, I was determined to get to know God as an intimate friend and the guide for my life. But how was I going to do this? How do we develop an intimate relationship with Jesus Christ?

One of the first keys to developing a relationship with Jesus is getting into His Word. In the books of the Bible—especially the stories of Jesus and the letters written by Paul and the other apostles—God Himself writes to us, letting us know what He thinks is important and telling us stories of all those through the years who have been courageous enough to draw close to Him and do His will. In getting into His Word, it is also good to get into Bible studies and sit under the teaching of others to learn what they know and how it has changed their lives. God has called us to need each other and learn from each other as fellow believers, and we need that constant interaction to make us stronger.

Of course, if we just stopped there, then we could let our faith lapse into religion and just go on what others say rather than knowing God for ourselves, so we also need to spend time talking to God ourselves in prayer. *Prayer is a two-way communication.* Not only do we need to spend time talking—but we also need to listen. We need to do more than present our requests and needs to God; we need to let His requests and needs touch our hearts. We need to let His passion and energy soak into our hearts.

Then we need to get into His presence. The Bible tells us that God inhabits the praises of His people (Ps. 22:3). That means that when His people gather together and lift their voices to Him in praise and worship, that act of worship creates room for Him to come and be with them. When we are willing to lay aside our own needs and desires for a time to come before God and sing our thanksgivings and praises to Him, it allows Him to fill us afresh with His Spirit, speak to us, and touch our lives.

It was in this way that God spoke to many in the Bible about their destinies. He came to Joseph in dreams and showed him where He would take him if he were willing to follow. God appeared to Moses in a burning bush and spoke to him. He came to David in his music and songs. To others in the Bible, He sent His messengers—prophets, teachers, and ministers—to show them God's will for their lives and to urge them to seek it for themselves.

For some, God speaks to their hearts in a "still, small voice" as He did to Elijah. It might be an impression, as it was with me when I felt Him telling me He wanted me to attend the university. The closer we draw to Him, and the more we learn to recognize His voice, the easier it will be for Him to speak to us directly and to guide us into the abundant life He wants for us.

I want you to understand that you can only do your part; you cannot force God's actions. Your part is to draw near to Him. When you do, you can be sure that He will draw near to you, but how He speaks to you is up to Him, not you. I know a lot of people looking for their own burning-bush type of experiences, seeking for Jesus or an angel to appear to them so that they can finally know that God is real and know His will for their lives. This kind of thinking can make you miss God. You may be looking for one kind of communication when God is using another way to speak to you. If someone calls your cell phone number, you cannot answer the call using someone else's phone.

I have heard more than one minister say that we can miss the *supernatural* by seeking the *spectacular*. We want a dream or a vision, but all God gives us is an impression, and we end up missing Him not because He is silent, but because we are trying to control the way He speaks to us.

2. Develop the natural gifts and abilities God has placed within you.

Yet sometimes when He gives us an impression in our hearts, we can be unsure that it is Him speaking to us. That also happened to me as I wondered if He really wanted me to go to college or not. So I plugged into the second level of clues to my destiny: develop the natural gifts and abilities I already had inside of me.

Never Too Late

Key #7

Diamonds are found hidden under thick layers of black coal deep within the earth. Your true wealth is hidden deep within you as well.

✠

The kingdom of God does not come with observation; nor will they say, "See here!" or "See there!" For indeed, the kingdom of God is within you.

—LUKE 17:20–21

If you don't feel like you know what your destiny is, and you are already pursuing God through His Word, prayer, and worship, then it is not a bad exercise to get a pen and paper and start listing the things you are good at and that you like to do. List the things that seem to come naturally to you. If you are good with kids, then God may have something for you working with children or young people.

If you like music and writing songs, your destiny may be as a worship leader or entertainer. If you are an artist, a good organizer, a pleasant person to talk with, or any of a number of other qualities, then those can also be clues to the destiny God has for you.

On the other hand, you can also make a list of things you don't like or that really bother you. Sometimes when we are not sure of our skills, these can be clues to what we are supposed to do. If the fact that there are hungry people in the world seems to bother you much more than it bothers everyone else around you, then perhaps God is calling you to be a missionary to work to stop hunger in poor or war-torn nations. If you abhor seeing people suffer sicknesses, perhaps you are destined to be a doctor. Slavery made Moses mad because God had destined him to be a deliverer.

The only time we see Jesus really angry in the Scriptures is when He turned the money changers' tables over because through their religious tradition they had turned their house of prayer into a shopping mall. Jesus had been called to end such empty religion. Sickness also upset Him, because He was called to be a healer. What you dislike or what makes you really angry may also be clues to your destiny. Recognize the areas you should steer clear of as you look for a job or position that fits what God has called you to do.

I see a lot of young people these days just getting out of college or high school and entering the work force looking for no more than "something that pays," only to end up a few months later complaining about their jobs or wondering if work is just not for them. Years later they feel they are wasting their lives. Too many think that work is a curse, but the truth is that it is not. Good work is actually a blessing. Look at what Solomon, the wisest man who ever lived, has to say about it:

As for every man to whom God has given riches and wealth, and given him power to eat of it, to receive his heritage and *rejoice in his labor* [work]—*this is the gift of God.*
—ECCLESIASTES 5:19, EMPHASIS ADDED

This verse says that finding work that we can rejoice in is a gift of God. Good, meaningful, purposeful work only comes, though, when we plug into our destinies.

3. Surround yourself with mentors who can help you find your destiny.

Last, if you still don't know your destiny, are you around others who are eager to help you find it? While I had men like Doug and other leaders at Living Word, I don't think I realized how much I needed them until years later. They had my best interests at heart as they taught me basic things like being in the Word every day. For example, Doug taught me that there was a chapter in the Book of Proverbs for every day of the month—if today is the seventh, then I will read chapter 7 of Proverbs sometime during the day; if it is the twenty-seventh, then I'll read chapter 27, and so on. Although I don't do this every day, when I find I have a lull in my day, this still comes to me, and I pick up my Bible and read the correct chapter for the day.

But Doug also did so much more than that for me. He let me hang around him and see what pursuing God was like. The Bible tells us that there was a whole group of discontented, disillusioned, and despairing men who came to follow David as their "life coach," and eventually they came to bear the title of "David's Mighty Men" as a result of pursuing God with him. Just like them, you need to be around others hungry for God and addicted to helping others know and follow Him.

It's Never Too Late

If you are ever going to find your destiny, you have to chase it almost as much as you chase God. You are also going to have to plug in with a body of believers dedicated to helping you find it.

Every person has two sides—sort of like Dr. Jekyll and Mr. Hyde. One is pregnant with destiny, and the other is trapped in identity. Which will you give way to? Though God ordains our destiny, it will never be realized unless we hook up with Him in making it happen. So chase God, check your heart, find mentors, and don't be surprised if you start seeing the fist-sized cloud of destiny start heading your way as the first indication of the rainstorms of blessings that are just ahead!

Six

Cultivate What God Has Put Within You

The kingdom of God does not come with observation; nor will they say, "See here!" or "See there!" For indeed, the kingdom of God is within you.

—Luke 17:20–21

ABOUT THE THIRD year after I was saved and after Doug had become an associate pastor at the church, our pastor decided to open a K–6 private Christian school. At this time I also began getting the leading in my heart that I was going to have a change in my employment. I was so confident of this, in fact, that I started telling everyone at the fitness center that I wasn't going to be there much longer. I told them God had better things for me, and

He was getting ready to open the door for me to leave. Thinking back on it now, they must have thought I was crazy! I am sure that "Zach, Zach, the Holy Ghost Maniac" was not the worst thing they thought of calling me.

One day the phone at my desk rang, and I picked it up to find myself talking to my pastor. Living Word had a couple of thousand members, so though I had been introduced to the pastor a couple of times by Doug, I can't say he knew me very well or that I was a friend of his. However, somehow he had heard I was an accounting major, and so he asked me, "Do you want to work for the church? I am starting a school, and I'll need a bookkeeper."

When I told him I didn't have a CPA license or even a degree yet, he told me it didn't matter. He said that he had a large accounting firm downtown that would be overseeing me, and he just needed someone he could trust in the office to handle the day-to-day business of the school.

When I hung up I shouted so loudly everyone on the floor must have heard me. People around the office couldn't believe that I had been shooting my mouth off about leaving, and then got a job offer without filling out any applications or even sending out any résumés. Just as I had told them, I was leaving to go work as an accountant for a new school, even though I didn't have a degree, a license, or any credentials or experience. I turned in my notice that same day and started getting my things together for my new job.

It was 1993 when I left the fitness center and started working in a ministry as the accountant. That is really the first time any sense of destiny touched my life. Though I still had no idea I would ever pastor, or even leave Baltimore, I did sense I would spend the rest of my life working in the church on some form of ministry team. I entered the job with a real sense of purpose. It was like nothing I had ever experienced before.

My pastor let me make my own schedule, so I could still fit in my classes. One of the best parts of that was that on Fridays I didn't go into the church at all; I went downtown to have our books checked and to be trained by what was the largest accounting firm owned by African Americans in Baltimore at the time. This was not only a working arrangement, but also more like an internship, even though it had nothing to do with college. They not only taught me everything I needed to know to run the books for the school, but also everything I needed to know to do any of the same accounting work that they did. I learned the software programs, the methods they used, everything. It was an incredible blessing.

This continued for nearly six months, and I learned so much. It was amazing. I thought it couldn't get any better, but then my pastor came to me and told me he was going to stop using the accounting firm downtown and make me the accountant over the entire church and everything that it did. I still didn't have my degree yet and was only twenty-three, but he was going to make me the chief financial officer of an organization that had a budget of roughly $8 million a year. In all my dreams as a drug dealer, it was more money than I thought I would ever be responsible for, but it was also so different. Whereas the drug dealing had been a counterfeit destiny—and meant to kill me, this was true destiny, and it was meant to give me life. It felt so different! God had taken what was in me and showed me my true destiny. I was so happy and yet still so hungry for more of what God had for me.

And it was only just the beginning.

What's in You?

If the destiny of God is in our hearts before we were even born, how is it that so many wander so aimlessly and purposelessly in our world today?

Generally, I have discovered this happens for three reasons:

1. A person grows frustrated and discouraged over the years chasing dead ends and finally loses hope of ever finding his or her destiny. As a result, he or she stops pursuing it.

2. The busyness of just living overwhelms a person so he or she spends life struggling day in and day out to survive, living paycheck to paycheck, grabbing what little satisfaction he or she can find along the way by settling for "good enough" rather than God's best.

3. A person is deluded into accepting a false world that seems to address his or her heart's desires, but which actually is just a close counterfeit of what would really give meaning to that person's life.

We have an entire world today filled with people who are in the midst of an identity crisis because they don't even know their own hearts. To be honest, though, it is not really a crisis of identity as much as it is a *crisis of destiny*.

The problem is that everyone seems to think that the answer is out there somewhere—if I can just be like that person, if I can just get that particular job, if I can just get into the right school, if I can just get the right car or house or clothes or whatever. While all those things can be nice and might have a place, they are never the answer. We must instead be true to what is in our hearts—what God put there—and then we will find the life we have always longed to live.

It is not about what we don't have and want to get; it is about what we already have and what we do with it.

For me, as I began to follow God, I thought I would never again have nice clothes, a nice house, or money in my pocket to enjoy. I did do without those things for some time, but only because I found something richer in following my destiny. Today I have the clothes, the house, and the money in my pocket, but I would trade them away again in a heartbeat if they came between me and accomplishing God's dreams in my heart. As a drug dealer I had money because I had basically stolen it—by selling drugs to people, I stole life from them. To tell the truth, money owned me—I had to do whatever it demanded so that I could have it. Today I have money because God has blessed me with it, and I put it to work to serve Him and what He has put in my heart. Before, the money that passed through my hands was always a curse; today, the money that passes through my hands is always a blessing.

The Bible tells us that what is in us is a blessing that was put there to glorify God and show His greatness. Before I was born, God put it in me to be good with numbers, to be good at talking with people and persuading them to do what is best, to manage businesses successfully, and to know how to handle money. One day, when God finally released me to be a pastor, all of these things would be working for His kingdom to bring others out of darkness. Yet Satan had played on those same abilities, gifts, and desires by calling me to be a drug dealer. His desire was to destroy me and everyone my life touched.

When I was born again, the gifts and talents I had before as a drug dealer didn't change. I was still good with numbers, at making businesses grow, at persuading people, and at handling money. But God had a better plan for these skills. He took what the devil had used in me to do evil and turned them to do good.

God Will Use Your Gifts to Prosper You

A lot of preachers today say that God wants us to be prosperous, but then all they talk about is money. Prosperity is so much more than money. There are a lot of rich people with hundreds of millions of dollars who don't have true prosperity—in fact, there are poor people who are closer to it than they are. Look at what John had to say about being prosperous:

> Beloved, I pray that you may prosper in all things and be in health, just as your soul prospers.
>
> —3 JOHN 2

Does John say that we should be financially prosperous? Sure. Money is definitely included in any list of "all things," but is that all John meant? No way. "That you may prosper in all things and be in health" talks about a lot more than money. But I want you to discover that the key is not *what prosperity is* as much as *how it comes*. Prospering in all things and in health doesn't come because we pursue those things; they come "*as your soul prospers.*" Another way to say this would be: "I pray that you prosper in all things and in health *in proportion* to how your soul prospers." In other words, if we work to prosper our souls, the other things will follow, not the other way around.

I want to be sure this concept is not confusing to you. Many people confuse *soul* and *spirit* because they are very much alike. But the Bible differentiates between them in several places. Our spirits are the part of us that is born again when we accept Jesus as Lord and Savior. Where before we were dead on the inside looking for life, now we are alive on the inside looking for ways to let that life overtake our entire being. We have a soul, which is our mind, will, emotions, and personality. When we are born again, our soul doesn't change as dramatically as our spirit does, but instead is redirected from death to life and must be developed and retrained to live that life.

For me, the first thing that happened was that God began to renew my mind with His Word and through my fellowship with Him in praise, prayer, and worship. When I began to pray about my feelings and desires, He didn't tell me they were wrong, but instead He directed me to go to school so that I could control them and make them a blessing to everyone I met instead of a curse. I had to learn how to run a legal business, basic accounting practices, plus a whole bunch of other things so that I could redirect the gifts, skills, and abilities in my soul to serve God and His purposes rather than my own lusts and Satan's destructive plans.

A lot of people come into a church to find fulfillment in their lives, and they are given instead a list of dos and don'ts to memorize and try to follow, as if Christianity were some game they could win by just not making any mistakes or incurring any penalties. But Jesus was never about legalism; instead, He is about abundant life. He isn't about suppressing our hearts' desires, but about fulfilling them in the best ways possible. He is all about helping us tap into the destiny He planted within each person and developing it to the fullest extent. And the major clues to your destiny are the skills, gifts, talents, abilities, and desires God has put within you.

A Rod, a Jar of Oil, a Little Boy's Lunch, and a Slingshot

When God came to people in the Scriptures to help them manifest their destinies, He didn't give them something new; instead, He asked them *what they already had.*

A rod

Look at this brief part of the conversation God had with Moses:

> Then Moses answered and said, "But suppose they will not believe me or listen to my voice, suppose they say, 'The LORD had not appeared to you.'" So the LORD said to him, "*What is that in your hand?*" He said, "A rod." And He said, "Cast it on the ground." So he cast it on the ground, and it became a serpent; and Moses fled from it. Then the LORD said to Moses, "Reach out your hand and take it by the tail" (and he reached out his hand and caught it, and it became a rod in his hand), "that they may believe that the LORD God of their fathers, the God of Abraham, the God of Isaac, and the God of Jacob, has appeared to you."
>
> —EXODUS 4:1–5, EMPHASIS ADDED

God didn't give something new to Moses to prove He had spoken to him; instead He used something with which Moses was very familiar. From that day forward, that rod would represent the power of God in many different ways, from swallowing up Pharaoh's serpents to splitting the Red Sea to bringing water out of a rock.

A jar of oil

Look at what God did through Elisha for a woman whose husband had left her in debt:

> A certain woman of the wives of the sons of the prophets cried out to Elisha, saying, "Your servant my husband is dead, and you know that your servant feared the LORD. And the creditor is coming to take my two sons to be his slaves." So Elisha said to her, "What shall I do for you? *Tell me, what do you have in the house?*" And she said, "Your maidservant has nothing in the house but *a jar of oil*." Then he said, "Go, borrow vessels

from everywhere, from all your neighbors—empty vessels; do not gather just a few. And when you have come in, you shall shut the door behind you and your sons; then pour it into all those vessels, and set aside the full ones."

—2 KINGS 4:1–4, EMPHASIS ADDED

You see, she was in a bad financial position. Her husband had died and left her in so much debt that the repo men weren't just after her car—they were going to take her two sons and sell them into slavery. She didn't have a job to work off her debt, and the situation must have looked hopeless. But when she came to Elisha, he gave her a command from the Lord to follow, so she went to do as he had commanded her to do:

So she went from him and shut the door behind her and her sons, who brought the vessels to her; and she poured it out.

—2 KINGS 4:5

She did what? She did what Elisha had told her to do. All she had was one little jar of oil, but in it was the answer to all of her financial problems.

Too many of us miss our blessing because we look at what we have through our human eyes and say, "This is just not enough to matter." We look at ourselves and say, "I don't have enough education," "I don't have the right education," "I didn't grow up in the right neighborhood," "I'm not smart enough," "I don't have enough money to start a business," "I don't have the time to help with that," "I don't have the right skills for a promotion," or any number of "can'ts" and "not enough ofs." Don't miss the blessing God has for you because you are looking at how little you have and not factoring in what God can do with even the smallest of things. Instead, listen for what He says you are to do with what you already have, because He can make a little a lot. Don't keep looking at what little you have

81

instead of letting God show you the potential He has locked inside your *little*. He has locked up five—or fifty!—more bottles of oil in that one little bottle of oil. He is just looking for someone who is willing to take the lid off. He is looking for someone to obey His command so that He can remove the limitations in the natural with His supernatural ability!

Nothing gets multiplied until it is worked.

Seeds don't grow unless they are put in the ground. Animals don't multiply if they are locked up in cages alone. Products don't produce revenues if they just sit on the production line or in the warehouse. An idea doesn't produce an income for the person who had it if it is not explored, researched, and put into action. Money never increases unless it is invested. It is not how little you have that counts; *it is what you do with what you have that matters!*

Look at what the widow did with her little jar of oil and God's commandment to her:

> So she went from him and shut the door behind her and her sons, who brought the vessels to her; and she poured it out. Now it came to pass, when the vessels were full, that she said to her son, "Bring me another vessel." And he said to her, "There is not another vessel." So the oil ceased.
>
> —2 KINGS 4:5–6

When did the oil stop? *When the last vessel was filled.* Who determined how many vessels were brought? *The widow and her sons, not God.* He didn't give her a number to gather other than "*do not gather just a few*," nor did the oil run out with vessels still left to fill. In other words, it would have filled as many vessels as she and her sons brought, right? The blessing was from the Lord, but the magnitude of the blessing was based on how much the widow and her sons were willing to work to gather vessels, not some predetermined amount set by God.

You couldn't see the magnitude of the blessing in the natural because it was supernatural. Somehow God made a connection between that little jar of oil and the eternal oil supply of heaven, and as long as there was something to pour the oil into, it would continue to flow. The oil did not stop until she ran out of things to pour it into!

Then when the miracle was over:

> She came and told the man of God. And he said, "Go, sell the oil and pay your debt; and you and your sons live on the rest."
>
> —2 Kings 4:7

Listen to how much God gave her. She had not only enough to pay her debt, but also to live on and take care of herself and her children *for the rest of her life*! Even when she died, her children would have some left over—all because she was bold enough to take the lid off of that bottle of oil and start pouring it out! God gives without measure, and if you don't put a limit on Him, He won't put a limit on you!

You see, God wants us to live with no lack. He doesn't want us calling the church to see if we can get some help to pay our light bill; He wants us to call the church to see if there are people we can help by paying *their* light bill! God is looking for people who want to live overflowing lives, because those are the only kind of people who will bless others when He blesses them. God is looking for pipelines of blessing, not holding tanks where the blessings will sit and stagnate.

A little boy's lunch

If that is not enough proof for you, look at what Jesus and the disciples did with a little boy's lunch:

83

When it was evening, His disciples came to Him, saying, "This is a deserted place, and the hour is already late. Send the multitudes away, that they may go into the villages and buy themselves food." But Jesus said to them, "They do not need to go away. You give them something to eat." And they said to Him, "We have here only five loaves and two fish."

—MATTHEW 14:15–17

Once again, we are dealing with something here that looks insignificant. It's small and doesn't look like enough. But look at what happens with that little bit:

He said, "Bring them here to Me." Then He commanded the multitudes to sit down on the grass. And He took the five loaves and the two fish, and looking up to heaven, He blessed and broke and gave the loaves to the disciples; and the disciples gave to the multitudes. So they all ate and were filled, and they took up twelve baskets full of the fragments that remained. Now those who had eaten were about five thousand men, besides women and children.

—MATTHEW 14:18–21

Jesus commanded the multitude to sit down on the grass. He took the five loaves and the two fishes, looked up to heaven, blessed them, broke them into pieces, gave the pieces to His disciples, and the disciples started handing them out to the multitude. Imagine the lesson for the disciples as they just kept handing out food from a couple of handfuls and watched as it never ran out. Then, as the people ate and shared the little bit each of them was given, it still never ran out! When everyone had been fed and was full, the disciples took baskets to gather the excess.

How many disciples were there? Twelve. How many baskets did they collect? *Twelve.* Again, the food didn't stop multiplying until the last person was full and the last basket was filled. I believe that had there been fifteen disciples, there would have been fifteen basketfuls left; had there been fifty disciples, there would have been fifty basketfuls!

Remember, when God makes a command that makes a demand on your faith and you obey, a power is released to accomplish whatever task is before you. Whatever we give to God and work as He tells us to will not stay the same. The real miracle didn't happen when they were passing it out, though—the miracle happened as soon as they took what they had and placed it in His hands.

A slingshot

When God called David to be king and he went to fight Goliath, he didn't accept Saul's generous offer of new armor and weaponry, but instead he fought with the same slingshot with which he had been chasing lions and bears away from his sheep for years. When Elijah came to the widow of Zaraphath because God had told him that she would feed him through the famine, God didn't make food appear before them so that they could eat it, but instead He multiplied the last handful of flour and few drops of oil she was willing to share with the man of God so that it lasted for many, many days. (See 1 Kings 17:8–16.)

Why does God do this? Because before you were born, He provided all the things you needed for health, prosperity, and living a meaningful life *within you in seed form.* It is your part to realize that you have them, to present them to God to use, then nurture them and work them. It is His job to multiply them, make them grow, and see that they bear healthy fruit in you so that you can use those fruits to bless others.

What are your dreams and desires? What are you good at? What do you like to do that makes you feel like you have something to offer others? It is very likely these are the things God has put within you that you will need to fulfill His call. They are there to give your life the purpose you need to have a fulfilled and rewarding life.

Never Doubt What Has Been Put Within You

Grammatically the difference is only an apostrophe and one letter, but there is really an earth-shattering difference between *"I can"* and *"I can't."*

It is true that the external world and the way that we are brought up greatly influences our lives. But one of the things that has always floored me is the difference between a kid who, despite growing up in a suburban, wealthy neighborhood, is convinced that life is too hard, the world is too evil, and there is really nothing he or she can do to make a difference and a kid who, although he lives in an inner-city ghetto, believes that despite the odds, life is only worth living if you make a positive impact in the lives of others, that there is nothing he can't overcome, and that good will always triumph as long as it never quits. If I asked you which you think would succeed despite their upbringing and family background, what would you say? Would it be the ghetto kid with the "I can" attitude or the wealthy kid with the "I can't" attitude?

In the midst of my rebellion, I was totally uncontrollable, but despite that, I always knew there were people who believed in me. Despite the fact that she had to force me out of her house to live with my father, the only thing that my mother ever said that still rings in my ears today is her constant words: "You're better than that, Zach; you're better than that." She didn't do this in a badgering way, and she wasn't like those moms always defending their sons even as they are being sentenced to death for murder, who say, "But he's a good boy! He didn't do anything wrong; he's a good boy!" No, my mother knew what I was doing was wrong, but she never let go of the fact that she believed I was better than that and was meant for more. She always believed that if I would just try, I could turn it all around.

I'm telling you, it makes a tremendous difference to know that someone believes in you like that.

And it makes a tremendous difference when someone prays for you as Doug prayed for me.

I say this for two reasons.

1. Never underestimate what God has put into your heart. Never accept that your destiny is "impossible" or that the gifts and abilities God put into you as He was crafting you in your mother's womb are "unimportant," "useless," or "not enough." There is a reason that He created you in the way He did, and it is never too late to start pursuing it. I can tell you from experience that there is no life that is as worth living as the one He has called you to live.

2. Never underestimate the power of your words in the life of another person or in praying for others. If your words are full of love, even if you are reprimanding them, they will know it; if your words are empty of love, even if you are praising them, they will know that, too. Even if everyone else thinks the person you are trying to help is hopelessly lost, what you say and what you pray can still make a difference.

Never Too Late

Key #8

The growth of a plant depends on its root system, on being planted in good soil, and on being given water and light. There is a seed in you that needs to grow.

✝

Grow in the grace and knowledge of our Lord and Savior Jesus Christ.

—2 PETER 3:18

It is never too late to turn a life around. But what you need to know is that there is good inside of you that is the true answer to what you are looking for.

For me, it started with my mother's words to a hardheaded rebel, and Doug's prayers for the worst case on his floor at work. Through those, God reached out and grabbed me and brought me into His light. Then He began to guide me toward His best for my life according to what was already in me before I was born. He helped me realize that my knack for numbers and business and speaking to people were all keys to my destiny in life. Then through giving those gifts back to God, using them to bring more people into His kingdom, and renewing my mind through the Word of God and attending a university, other areas of my life began to bear fruit. I had a drive and passion to do more. My collections job prospered. People started being able to trust me rather than wanting to kill me.

God was doing incredible things in my life, but better was still to come.

I think it was only around this time that I began to realize what had happened in my life. God had destined me for great things. Was I brave enough to let Him work them out in me?

Part Three

**Guard Your Turf;
Protect Your Seedlings**

Seven

True or False?

Test all things; hold fast what is good.
Abstain from every form of evil.
— *1 Thessalonians 5:21–22*

A s THE CFO for Living Word Christian Center, I was now making a very good salary—more money than anyone in my family had ever made—so I decided to move out of my mother's place and find my own. After some looking, I found a beautiful, big house in a nice neighborhood I liked, so I bought it. It was amazing how far I had come in such a short time.

Everything that I had tried to obtain through the devil's system I had now been blessed with through God's system. At the same time, there were so many other things that came with it that I treasured even more. I had a peace and joy in my life that I had never experienced before. This was a time when God's presence was so real and so sweet in my life, and there was so much to do. I had such a feeling of life-changing and world-changing purpose in my life, it was hard to think of too much else. I was in the middle of so many things of such great importance, God was using me for just what He had called me to be, and now He was also blessing me with great relationships in my life. Over the next couple of years I would start dating, get engaged to, and eventually marry Riva Jennings, who is still my loving wife and co-laborer in everything I do today.

You see, it is possible to have an abundance of stuff and still be bankrupt in heaven. It is possible to be head rich and heart poor—physically wealthy and spiritually destitute. It is part of the deceptive trap of the devil, and he can play it either way. His first plan is that we would fall for the trap of physical wealth, thinking that is all we really need to feel happy. When you fall for this, money and stuff become your primary object of worship. You will do anything to get them—lie, steal, cheat, and even sell people drugs that will kill them in order to get that *stuff*. Before you know it, you have built a cell like that little room in my dream around yourself that you can't get out of, and if it doesn't kill you, it will keep you serving it for the rest of your life.

There is no worse taskmaster than money and material possessions, whether you have a little of it or a lot of it—whether you live alone with billions in a penthouse like Howard Hughes or live from paycheck to paycheck, hand-to-mouth like those in poverty do. It will steal your life and the life of those around you. It will possess almost all of your thought life and sap your physical and mental health through ulcers, heart disease, depression, or any of a number of other stress-related ailments.

Never Too Late

Key #9

Seek the wisdom of God for man, not man for the wisdom of God.

✝

Get wisdom! Get understanding!
Do not forget, nor turn away from the words of my mouth.
Do not forsake her, and she will preserve you;
Love her, and she will keep you.
Wisdom is the principal thing;
Therefore get wisdom.

—Proverbs 4:5–7

If Satan can't sell you on his bill of goods after you have found Jesus, then he will try to push you in the exact opposite direction—where you believe that nothing counts but spiritual riches. Now this is a little more than half true—if I had to make a choice between spiritual wealth and physical wealth, I would say spiritual is more important, but God has wired us for both. We can never truly live the life God has given us to its fullest without more than enough both spiritually *and* physically. God doesn't want us poor in either area.

If we are willing to be religious, however, Satan will try to sell us on the idea that spiritual wealth is all that is important, and that only the poor can be truly holy. We will live to follow the dictates of a legalistic system of religion that often has very little to do with knowing God. We will feel unworthy of and reject material blessings because they are "of this world and unworthy of heaven."

The devil does this to keep Christians out of positions of power and influence where they can expand God's kingdom on the earth. Wealth is really just a measure of ability. The wealthier you are, the more you are able to do. Extreme Donald-Trump/Bill-Gates-type wealth builds skyscrapers, event centers, and transit systems; extreme Book-of-Acts-type wealth heals bodies and souls and renews human spirits. Both together transform nations. But of course, Satan doesn't want us transforming nations, so if he can keep us in one extreme or the other, then he can keep us powerless and ineffective, and he can manipulate the world without our interference.

God has wired us to live in both the material and spiritual world as blessings, and one without the other can leave us empty and keep us from fulfilling the dreams God has put in our hearts. The trick is, how do we live in both?

The answer is both simple and difficult at the same time: *seek Jesus first above all things*. As Jesus Himself put it:

> Therefore do not worry, saying, "What shall we eat?" or "What shall we drink?" or "What shall we wear?" For after all these things the Gentiles seek. For your heavenly Father knows that you need all these things. But seek first the kingdom of God and His righteousness, and all these things shall be added to you.
>
> —MATTHEW 6:31–33

This is simple in that there is just one thing to do—and Jesus really does want to be found by us. He wrote us a lot of letters and provided a lot of teaching in His Word to show us the way. He has sent us His Holy Spirit to guide and direct our every step, has given us His authority over those things that would keep us from His abundant life, and offers His presence and power to us when we praise and worship Him.

It is difficult in that Satan has aligned the entire world to thwart the kingdom of God. He feeds half-truths into churches so that people fall into extremism or settle for too little. He attacks faith with accusations of everything from questioning the validity of its sources to calling those who practice truth bigoted, corrupt, and greedy. Then he has also created an incredible network of counterfeits that promise to give us what God truly wants us to have—wealth, love, acceptance, sexual satisfaction, joy, and so many other good things—but instead empty our souls and lead to death.

In one way or another he robs us of our fathers so that we have to look to the world for images of how to find success and fulfillment. He replaces the joy of being married with everything from promiscuity to pornography; peace with drug highs and entertainment; good work and purpose with greed, hopelessness, crime, and corruption—turning all God has meant for good and completion into idols that erode life instead of give it.

It is essentially the same three temptations Satan offered Jesus in the wilderness. Look for a minute at the story:

> Then Jesus was led up by the Spirit into the wilderness to be tempted by the devil. And when He had fasted forty days and forty nights, afterward He was hungry. Now when the tempter came to Him, he said, "If You are the Son of God, command that these stones become bread." But He answered and said, "It is written, 'Man shall not live by bread alone, but by every word that proceeds from the mouth of God.'"
>
> Then the devil took Him up into the holy city, set Him on the pinnacle of the temple, and said to Him, "If You are the Son of God, throw Yourself down. For it is written: 'He shall

give His angels charge over you,' and, 'In their hands they shall bear you up, lest you dash your foot against a stone.'" Jesus said to him, "It is written again, 'You shall not tempt the LORD your God.'"

Again, the devil took Him up on an exceedingly high mountain, and showed Him all the kingdoms of the world and their glory. And he said to Him, "All these things I will give You if You will fall down and worship me." Then Jesus said to him, "Away with you, Satan! For it is written, 'You shall worship the LORD your God, and Him only you shall serve.'" Then the devil left Him, and behold, angels came and ministered to Him.

—MATTHEW 4:1–11

What did you see in reading this passage? When I look at it, I see that the first temptation was one *to fulfill physical appetites*. While the example here is breaking His fast—His vow before God—for the sake of food, I think it can apply to any compromise we are willing to make to satisfy our physical hungers in a way that violates God's ways, whether that be hunger, sex, or meeting any other kind of physical desire.

What was Jesus' answer? "I will do things the way God has instructed me to, not the way you offer to get these things."

The second temptation was to believe there were *no consequences for reckless or selfish actions*. Satan even tried to justify it from the Word! "Throw yourself off of this tower without a parachute, and God will catch you! You won't suffer for it, and what a ride it will be on the way down!"

Jesus' answer? "Don't try God's patience. He will not protect us from our own foolishness forever, especially if we know better."

The last temptation? "If you will worship me—in other words, *live your life my way by rejecting God's ways*—then you can have all the material wealth and power the world has to offer."

Again, Jesus' answer? "Get out of here! This isn't even yours to give! I know the only fulfillment in life comes from following and worshiping God alone, not you!"

And, frustrated and beaten, Satan left.

Do we want the same in our lives?

The Eyes Have It!

There is another lesson for us in the example from Jesus: How did Satan present these temptations to Jesus? "*See* those rocks?" "*Look* out from this tower…" "Let me *show* you the nations and their glory…" Every one of the temptations started with Satan showing Jesus something. He did the same thing when he showed me the drug dealers on the corner in front of the arcade and whispered in my ear, "See those guys? They have the 'good life'! Follow them, be like them, conform to their identities, and you can have it all, too!"

What did the devil do with Adam and Eve to tempt them to eat from the tree of the knowledge of good and evil?

> So when the woman *saw* that the tree was good for food, that it
> *was pleasant to the eyes*, and a tree desirable to make one wise,
> she took of its fruit and ate. She also gave to her husband with
> her, and he ate.
>
> —GENESIS 3:6, EMPHASIS ADDED

Again, Satan got her to look, and when she did, it was simply a question of "Why do what God says? There it is, take it!" And she did, and then turned and gave it to Adam.

Satan still tempts the same way today. He still says, "Look at that. Doesn't it look good? Why wait to have it? Just go get it! Do it your own way; why should you listen to anyone else?" You don't believe me? How often have you seen something—even on television

99

or in an ad—and said, "Oh, I wish I had that." Would the temptation have come to lust after that thing if you hadn't placed your eyes on it in the first place?

Think about that for a minute. What does pornography do? "See that naked woman? Isn't she fine? Why don't you just go get you one like that? Why should you have to wait to be married?" But he doesn't get you to look at it in porn first; he slips it to you in television commercials and on shows saying, "Isn't this good stuff? Don't you want to see a little more?" And little by little he takes us to right where he wants us to be, either destroying our chances to have a proper relationship with our future wives or else destroying the marriage we already have.

What about those drug dealers on the corner? "See those guys? See how cool they look in all those brand-new clothes? You can be just like them; all you have to do is do what they do, and you can have what they have!"

Satan traps us with imagery, and then he gets us to try to identify with it. If he can get us to worship that image and want to have it no matter what, then he can slowly lead us down the trail to death without breaking a sweat.

You see, we don't get trapped by evil; we get trapped by *good*. You don't bait a trap with something the animal wouldn't want; you bait it with something tasty and good. Religion tries to say that the good offered in such traps is evil, but it's not. That's perverting it the other way. The bait is never "Do this and you will be miserable all of your life," but "Look at this—isn't it good? Don't you want it for yourself?" The answer is always *yes*, and then the evil comes not in wanting to have that thing, but in the way we are willing to get it. Now, of course, there are some things that are bad to want, like your neighbor's spouse, house, or car, but God has no problem with you enjoying and finding satisfaction with your own!

Jesus escaped Satan's temptation because He knew what the Word said and knew God wasn't a liar because of His relationship with Him. When Satan said, "Look at these things; don't you want them?" His answer was, "Sure, I want them, but I am going to get them God's way, not yours! Because God's ways bring life and yours bring death. Go away and stop bothering me."

Everything I had wanted as a boy, God gave me when I followed after Him with all of my heart. Everything I had gotten as a boy was taken away from me and was a trap set to kill me. Everything God has given me can never be taken away, and life and peace come also.

I thought I had finally arrived. I had more than I had ever hoped for, and I thought at the time I would be content to live with that, working for that church and ministry for the rest of my life. Little did I suspect, though, that God had so much more for me, and this was just the beginning. But there was also more He had to teach me before I would be ready for it.

I once heard a preacher say, "God loves you too much to leave you the way you are."

That is so, so true. It wasn't long before He began working on me again to lead me into even more of the abundant life He wanted me to have.

Eight

Watch the Door

Keep your heart with all diligence,
For out of it spring the issues of life.

—Proverbs 4:23

THE YEAR 1994 was a very eventful year for me. It was the year I graduated from the university, the year I got married, and the year a scandal broke out involving one of the leaders in our church. When the news hit the front page of the Saturday "Living" section of a major Baltimore newspaper, the effects were disastrous. Our congregation decreased by about 60 percent in two months. Attendance went from a couple of thousand every Sunday to less than a thousand.

As a result of this decrease, income decreased as well, and all of the executives who remained at the church—which, by then, included myself as well as Douglas and some others—took immediate salary cuts. My wife, who was personnel director at the church, was laid off. Not only that, but the executive staff of the church got paid last, so if the church had barely enough income to cover the regular expenses and support staff salaries, it meant we would not be paid that week, which happened several times. I did have some other income from a business I had started on the side called Church Financial Services, which did the books for smaller congregations who didn't want the expense of a full-time accountant, but it was not enough to cover our regular monthly expenses, so things got tight quickly.

In response to this, our pastor's pastor—the man he looked to as his mentor—took our pastor away with him to Africa for two months in order to get him away from the media circus and help him figure out what he needed to do to help the church recover. While he was away, Douglas, myself, and another man, who were all that was left of the executive team, took charge of the church and did our best to keep things from completely falling apart.

Who Let the Snake in?

It is a sad thing to realize, but no matter how long we have walked with God, it cannot keep us from stumbling if we don't watch our steps and guard our hearts. What we let in, what we fix our eyes upon, matters. It is up to each of us to keep our eyes focused on Jesus as we push forward toward Him, but also to shut out and strip away the things that could hold us back or trip us up.

In the Garden of Eden, Adam really had only two things he needed to worry about as far as staying on track with God: the tree of the knowledge of good and evil, and the door to the garden. But Adam let his guard down and let the serpent into the garden, otherwise they never would have heard it speak to them as it wrapped itself around one of the limbs of the tree of knowledge. Did Adam know? Of course he did. He was the one who named all of the animals, and he gave the serpent the name *serpent* because that name came from the word *enchanter*. He knew it was a beguiling creature that needed to be watched. When he let it roam freely in the garden, he was opening himself up for a downfall.

Look at the story again briefly and see if you notice anything new in it:

> Now the serpent *was more cunning than any beast of the field which the* LORD *God had made.* And he said to the woman, "Has God indeed said, 'You shall not eat of every tree of the garden'?" And the woman said to the serpent, "We may eat the fruit of the trees of the garden; but of the fruit of the tree which is in the midst of the garden, God has said, 'You shall not eat it, nor shall you touch it, lest you die.'"
>
> Then the serpent said to the woman, "You will not surely die. For God knows that in the day you eat of it your eyes will be opened, and you will be like God, knowing good and evil." So when the woman *saw* that the tree was good for food, that it was pleasant to the eyes, and a tree desirable to make one wise, she took of its fruit and ate. She also gave to her husband *with her*, and he ate.
>
> —GENESIS 3:1–6, EMPHASIS ADDED

Notice a couple of things here. First of all, before the story even begins, we are told that the serpent was a cunning creature. As I already said, this is why Adam named it *serpent*. He knew it was not to be completely trusted. Second, the serpent's words never hit home with Eve until she looked at the fruit herself and saw it in the light of how the serpent presented it to her. Certainly the fruit was a good thing, but it *was not to be taken without permission*. The temptation was to doubt the consequences of disobedience. "You won't die!" the serpent told her, and she believed him. Then when she took the fruit and ate it, her spirit inside of her was struck a fatal blow and died in that instant, even though her physical body lived on.

That wasn't much different from what I was told when I started selling drugs. "You won't get arrested," the other guys told me, "and even if you do, you will only spend about three months in juvie, and then they will let you out. And when you get out, your rep on the street will be that much bigger because you served time and came back tougher for it." They also told me, "If you just use the little stuff—smoke a little weed, snort a little coke every now and then—you won't get addicted. It's just fun. With all the money you are making, you deserve to enjoy yourself some too, don't you?"

Yet these were lies too, and when I believed them, I acted accordingly. And though I didn't die physically that day, all of these things were aimed at killing me, and probably would have before I was twenty if God hadn't stepped in to save me.

But there is also one other thing I want you to notice in this story. That is the two words, *with her*—"She gave also to her husband *with her*." In other words, during this entire conversation, Adam had (I believe) been standing right there next to Eve and listened to the whole thing! Why didn't he speak up? Why didn't he grab the snake by the neck and throw it out of the garden? Why didn't he counter what it said with what God had really told him? Instead, he just stood there and watched his wife make the biggest mistake in the history of the world, and then joined her in it.

What's in Your Garden?

People don't wake up one day, go to a hotel, take their clothes off, and then jump into bed with someone else all by accident. That might be kind of a blunt way to put it, but it is still true. It comes in a process of compromises and through a series of wrong decisions that no one sees because they are blinded by their selfish desires.

There is a whole world headed for hell today—and many people are living hell on earth—because they think they will never have to pay for their sins. Unfortunately, there are too many Christians today missing God's best for their lives either because of such sins or because they are accepting some other lie that is keeping away what God is trying to get to them.

What are you tolerating in your life that no one else even knows about?

Are you doing something with those prescription drugs that your doctor never prescribed for you to do? What about the Web sites you visit that you don't want the rest of your family to find out about? Are you making up lame excuses for hanging a little bit longer after the service to talk with Sister Renee or Brother Marcus and looking to get something from them you feel your spouse isn't giving you anymore? Are you letting your eyes linger a little too long on certain "attributes" of their bodies as they walk away? Are you trying to squeeze out more pay on your job for less work? Are you looking for ways to be "on the clock" but "out to lunch" at the same time?

If so, you are letting serpents roam your garden—and it won't be long before you get bitten.

Never Too Late

Key #10

In the Old Testament days, they strapped small, lighted candles to their ankles to light their way in the darkness of night to prevent them from stumbling over rocks or treading on snakes. The Word of God is a lamp that illuminates your pathway in life.

☩

Your word is a lamp to my feet
And a light to my path.

—Psalm 119:105

In fact, the biggest blessing that can happen to you in the middle of such sin is that *you will be found out*. Otherwise, how else will you ever be brought to account and repent? You think God's leaving you in your secret sin is going to do you any good?

You may think you aren't hurting anybody else with what you are doing, but what about those you are not helping because you are letting some selfish desire keep you from your destiny? Certainly, fulfilling our destinies is a blessing to us, but if that is all you are in it for, you are really missing the best part. Fulfilling our destinies also changes the life of every person we touch. There may be millions of people out there counting on your destiny, and if you gamble it away in some pursuit for temporary pleasure, everyone loses big, *including you*.

Of course, you don't have to wait for God to bless you by exposing you to the world; you can repent now and avoid public embarrassment. If you don't, God is going to bless you the best way He can anyway, and that means that those things you do in darkness will be brought into the light!

The key is keeping our hearts fully in His hands all the time.

Seeds Always Start to Grow in Darkness

You can keep seeds on your desk, in your drawer, on a shelf, in a barn, or in a million other places, and they will never do anything but be seeds. They may have the potential to grow up into redwoods that will last for hundreds of years and reach high into the sky, or they may have the potential to grow into fruit-bearing trees that can feed millions. Many people wonder about how many seeds are in an apple, but few wonder how many apples—or apple trees and orchards—are in a seed. Yet seeds can remain dormant for decades and never accomplish anything if they are never put into the soil—buried in the dark—and watered. Only then will they begin to sprout and start to grow into what they are supposed to become.

Most great things start when no one else is looking. Many people think that what they are doing when no one else is watching doesn't matter, but it does. Great things often start because someone pays attention to the little details no one else cares about. I can tell you, the person who goes home every night to crash on the couch in front of the TV and the person who goes home and opens his or her Bible to read or to pray will have very different results in life, even though they start in the same place. This, of course, doesn't mean you can never watch TV, but if that is what you live for, then you are headed to a very different place than someone living to hear God's voice so he can obey it.

This principle works for both good and bad seeds, however. Weed seeds also thrive in darkness and when no one is looking. We need to be diligent in pulling them up as soon as we notice them and doing what we can to be sure they don't get planted in the first place.

What happens in the dark, when no one else is looking, matters.

Keep bad things from taking root, and they will never see the light of day. Be diligent in nurturing the good things even when no one else notices, and the day will come when everyone can appreciate your diligence in doing right.

Look at what Jesus said about the power of faith, even though it starts as the smallest of seeds:

> If you have faith as a mustard seed, you will say to this mountain, "Move from here to there," and it will move; and nothing will be impossible for you.
>
> —MATTHEW 17:20

> To what shall we liken the kingdom of God? Or with what parable shall we picture it? It is like a mustard seed which, when it is sown on the ground, is smaller than all the seeds on earth; but when it is sown, it grows up and becomes greater than all herbs, and shoots out large branches, so that the birds of the air may nest under its shade.
>
> —MARK 4:30–32

God means for the call of your heart—the seed of destiny of His kingdom inside of you—to come to full growth so that others may rest in the shade of what He has done in your life. Greatness and destiny are already in you; conform to them and not the outside identities the world is trying to use to smother all God wants to do through you.

Nine

Know the Season

[God] has saved us and called us with a holy calling, not according to our works, but according to His own purpose and grace which was given to us in Christ Jesus before time began.

—*2 Timothy 1:9*

AT THE END of the summer of 1994, our pastor came back from his time in Africa with a plan to revitalize the church. This proved more difficult in practice than in theory, however. It was still only a few months after the newspaper article, and the name of the church was still scandalized in the public eye.

Some who know about those times have asked me why I didn't leave when the scandal hit (because in the end it reflected on every member of the executive counsel through association, though we had nothing to do with the incident). Several congregation members and support staff members "got off the sinking ship"; why didn't I? The simple reason is that by then, my personal prayer life was much stronger, and I was hearing God's voice more and more—and He simply didn't tell me to leave. In fact, I felt led to do just the opposite, so I stayed to do what I could to keep the church going. Looking back, if I had bolted with all the others, I wouldn't be where I am today. God didn't cause the scandal, but He did use it to test my faithfulness in a storm, and it seems that through following His leading in a dark time, I passed the test.

When our pastor returned, the first thing he did was change the name of the church, but that did little good since we were still meeting in the same building. Then he decided to start sending people out to plant churches in other parts of the country. If his immediate body was still reeling from the scandal, he would do as they did in Jerusalem when persecution came there—scatter those still faithful throughout the rest of the land. The first to go out was Douglas, who went to Phoenix, Arizona, where he is still pastoring today. In the coming months others would go out to Jackson, Mississippi; Atlanta, Georgia; Boston, Massachusetts; Raleigh, North Carolina; Las Vegas, Nevada; and Houston, Texas.

Then came the knock on my door. My pastor met with me, and, after some small talk, he put the question to me directly: "Zach, do you want to go out and plant a church?" Though I should have foreseen this, I was instead floored. I was married and starting a family. We had a nice home in a nice neighborhood, the church seemed to be stabilizing somewhat again, and my outside business, Church Financial Services, was doing better than ever. When he asked me to go out, suggesting that I leave behind all I had in Baltimore, my first thought was to rebuke the devil for ever putting such an idea into his head!

To me, I already had everything that I had ever hoped for—everything I felt God had promised me—and in my mind any attempt to take it away must have been of the devil. Yet in the next few months, all of that would change. It appeared that destiny had more waiting for me someplace else.

The Changing of the Season

Some people might think that I decided to leave that church because of what had happened with the scandal, the change in salary, or the like, but the truth of the matter is that when he asked me to go out, I had absolutely no interest in leaving. I was comfortable with my lifestyle and had outside income to provide for my family should more financial problems hit the church, yet what I found happening was that something in me started to change. Where I had been so comfortable before, I grew restless. Everything that had felt so right before started to feel out of sync. God was changing my heart, and in doing so was reawaking the true destiny He had for me. He seemed to think that I was ready for the next level.

You see, just as there are phases or seasons in our lives as we grow up, there are also phases or seasons in realizing our God-given destinies. Just because God had called me to go to a university to learn, that didn't mean I would be in that university for the rest of my life.

As I look back now, in fact, I see God was trying to build into me during that period things that would be important to my destiny later on. He told me to go to the university so that I could learn the self-discipline to study as well as managing my time because I had to balance classes, church, and working thirty or more hours a week. He called me to be the church accountant on the executive board of the church so that I could be trained in leadership and operating a ministry. There were lessons I needed to learn in each of those areas that help me every day in managing the life-changing church I am in today. Had I not applied myself fully to them, I don't think I would be where I am today. Had I let other things distract me or had I not fully applied myself, then I doubt I would be doing what I am now or that it would be as successful. Just as someone who never graduates from high school or earns a GED can't go to college, so too if we fail to "pass" the tests of the season we are in, it can keep us from moving on to the next.

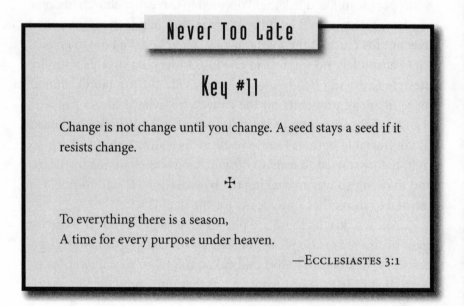

Never Too Late

Key #11

Change is not change until you change. A seed stays a seed if it resists change.

✠

To everything there is a season,
A time for every purpose under heaven.
—ECCLESIASTES 3:1

We have to realize that as the seasons change, so will many other things in our lives. God gives us a grace to be in the place we are supposed to be, but when the time to be in that place ends, so will the grace. If you are six years old and in first grade, all is fine, but if you are fifteen and in first grade, things will be awkward and out of place. However, none of these natural things will matter if it is where God wants you to be. I was older than most of my classmates in college and took five years to graduate rather than four, but I had God's grace to be right where I was. However, when it was time for me to move on, that grace began to lift, and I became restless.

Though I loved Baltimore and working as CFO for the church, and was very comfortable with it all, when the grace lifted to be there, though none of the circumstances changed, I began to feel out of place. Little things that were of no significance before started to bug me. It was part of God's gentle nudging to get me back on the track to the destiny to which He had called me, even though at the time I had no idea what it was.

In this we need to also realize that as we change seasons, we can also change relationships. What was right for one period of our life may not have the same place in the next. This is why I call some people and occupations in our lives scaffolding and rocket-boosters.

Scaffolding is put up while you are building, but once the building is done, you take it down. Some people are scaffolding—so are some jobs or schooling. There is a time to be in college and a time to graduate just as there was a time for me to be an accountant and another time for me to be a pastor. Some people are in your life while you are being built up and leave after that. Some you will still look to for wisdom years later even though you are in different cities, different states, or on different continents.

Some people and experiences are rocket boosters. They launch you, and then at a certain point drop off and disappear. Sometimes you have to push them off, because that which was a help at the beginning may turn to a hindrance or a weight later on, just as a rocket gets rid of empty fuel tanks so that it is not weighed down by them, even though they were essential in the initial launching.

Part of changing seasons is also discerning what to keep and what to let go of; what to continue doing and what to stop doing; and what is essential now and what should be left behind or dismantled and put away until another season.

Destiny tends to come in pieces, like the puzzle I spoke about in the introduction. We get a piece or two at a time, focusing on one part of the whole at a time, and only God knows what the full "picture on the box" looks like. If He chooses to, He can show us the whole picture as He did to Joseph, but also like Joseph, that tends to mean there is a very tough road ahead. The more typical experience is like that of Abraham, whom God told, "Get out of your country, from your family and from your father's house, to a land that I will show you" (Gen. 12:1). God didn't show him the land until he started walking. As Abraham journeyed, God led him a step at a time.

Why? Because God loves us so much that He wants to take the journey with us. He wants daily, step-by-step fellowship with us. If we draw near to Him, He will show us exactly what we need to do even if we don't understand why. For me, in the season of storminess in our Baltimore church, that meant staying put. The next season would be one of leaving the city where I was born and where my family lived to follow God to a new land.

As I started working at the church in Baltimore and continued to learn how to pray from Doug, I began to realize that not only does God still talk to His people if we will listen, but also if we will really pursue Him, we will discover that He will talk to us through His Word and in our hearts as much as the other people with whom we live and work talk to us daily. In fact, God longs to talk with us and fellowship with us all the time. The trouble, of course, is in getting practiced enough in hearing Him that we can discern His voice from our own. This can't be done by just taking ten or fifteen minutes a day to pray. You have to really get in and pursue Him until you get through to the Spirit in your prayer life.

Many times when we are young in the Lord, He will speak to us from time to time without us really pressing into prayer, but God expects us to grow. There are things that are permissible when we are young in the Lord—in one season of our life—that need to be developed for us to grow toward fullness in the next season of life. Learning to pray more fervently on a regular basis and learning to discern His voice are parts of that growth process. This will take you into what I like to call "pockets of success" such as I experienced when I followed God's voice and enrolled in the university or when I started working at the church. It is sort of like the changing from one type of soil into the best type of soil that Jesus discusses in the parable of the sower.

What Kind of Soil Are You?

In the Gospels of Mark and Luke in the Bible, Jesus tells what is called the *parable of the sower*, which discusses the potential levels of fruitfulness in our lives. But the name of the parable is a bit misleading to me: I don't think it is really so much about the sower or even the seed, but more about the types of soil that receives the seeds. Take a look at the story as Jesus tells it in Mark and see if you understand what I mean:

> Behold, a sower went out to sow. And it happened, as he sowed, that some seed fell by the wayside; and the birds of the air came and devoured it. Some fell on stony ground, where it did not have much earth; and immediately it sprang up because it had no depth of earth. But when the sun was up it was scorched, and because it had no root it withered away. And some seed fell among thorns; and the thorns grew up and choked it, and it yielded no crop. But other seed fell on good ground and yielded a crop that sprang up, increased and produced: some thirtyfold, some sixty, and some a hundred.
>
> —MARK 4:3–8

As Jesus goes on to explain a few verses later, the sower in this story represents the minister, preacher, teacher, or even Jesus Himself who sows the *seed*—the Word of God—into the lives of others. Notice that the sower throws his seed everywhere regardless of where he or she goes. The sower doesn't only throw it on the carefully plowed and fertilized land, but in the highways and byways as well—on the sidewalk, on the roadsides, everywhere the sower goes.

You see, the sower has absolute confidence in the Word and its potential. The promises of God are true whether someone lets them grow in their lives or not. The sower knows that the Word can change things wherever it goes *depending on the type of soil it lands in*. If this is true, then the sower must also believe that any type of soil can change and become fruitful if it wants to. So the question becomes, "What kind of soil are you?" And if you are the wrong kind, "Are you willing to make the changes to become the good ground where the Word of God can produce thirty, sixty, or one hundred times what was sown into it?"

Look at what Jesus explained about these four types of soil:

And these are the ones by the wayside where the word is sown. When they hear, Satan comes immediately and takes away the word that was sown in their hearts. These likewise are the ones sown on stony ground who, when they hear the word, immediately receive it with gladness; and they have no root in themselves, and so endure only for a time. Afterward, when tribulation or persecution arises for the word's sake, immediately they stumble. Now these are the ones sown among thorns; they are the ones who hear the word, and the cares of this world, the deceitfulness of riches, and the desires for other things entering in choke the word, and it becomes unfruitful. But these are the ones sown on good ground, those who hear the word, accept it, and bear fruit: some thirtyfold, some sixty, and some a hundred.

—MARK 4:15–19

Wayside soil

The first type is the "wayside soil." This is sort of like throwing seeds onto cement—it just lies there to get eaten by the birds. This type of soil represents people whose hearts have been so hardened by sin and self-centeredness that they can't even receive the Word into them, and it bounces off like a basketball dropped on a gym floor. These people have been blinded and deceived by sin to such a point that the truth doesn't even register with them anymore. The Bible says that "their own conscience [has been] seared with a hot iron" (1 Tim. 4:2). Before the Word can be fruitful in such a person's life, they must repent and ask God to give them a new heart that is not made of concrete but of flesh that can hear, receive, and bear fruit from the truth it hears.

Rocky soil

The second type of soil is the "rocky soil." On the surface, these people look wonderful. They sing and praise God loudly during worship services, take notes as the preacher speaks, attend all the meetings they can, and to many seem to be everything a church member should be. Yet inside of themselves they have no depth. Just beneath the surface are rocks that keep the Word of truth from ever really taking root in their lives. These rocks could be past hurts that have never been dug up through prayer and forgiveness. They may be secret sins such as viewing pornography, racism, stealing when no one is looking, alcohol or drug abuse, or any of a million other little things that they refuse to get free from. They may be false beliefs or a legalism that hinders them from moving forward. It could also be a mind-set such as always playing the victim instead of being a victor, not seeing themselves as worthy of the things God wants to do in their lives, or being codependent with someone trapped by some form of abuse or self-destructive behavior.

To be truly fruitful, we need to dig these things out in prayer, fellowship with other believers who really care about us, and sometimes even seek Christian counseling for ourselves or our families. Until these "below the surface" issues are resolved, we will never have the depth required for God's Word to do all it can in our lives. "Rocky soil" people appear to be doing well on the outside, but when persecution or scandal comes, they fall away from the truth, because their faith was based more on looking good than on living good.

Thorny soil

The third type of soil is the "thorny soil." The thorny soil is similar to the stony soil in that the Word in their lives is hindered. But instead of the things within them keeping the roots from going deep, it is the things from without that choke the seed. Weeds and bramble bushes grow in them that don't leave any room for the Word to flourish. Jesus called these "the cares of this world, the deceitfulness of riches, and the desires for other things." Some people get so caught up with their jobs and increasing their paychecks that they stop going to church or taking the time to pray and study the Word so that they can grow. Others pick up social and political concerns to the point that they consume all of their time and pull them away from their true destiny. Others work to amass material possessions and get caught up in the physical part of prosperity, missing out on the spiritual prosperity Jesus called "true riches." They get so caught up with secondary things in life that they miss the primary importance of seeking God's kingdom and His righteousness above everything else. They major on minors and miss all that God has for them, because their priorities are out of whack.

This is perhaps the hardest type of soil to change from because it can seem so right. God does want us to prosper, and He has no trouble with us having nice things, but when the nice things start to have us and we are more ruled by making our next payment on our bigger house, big-screen television, or new boat than we are by doing God's will, then we are being choked by thornbushes. If we are so caught up in a righteous cause—doing the work of the Lord—that we forget the Lord of the work, then we are being smothered by weeds. If we are so caught up in the business of twenty-first-century life that we never have time to be quiet before the Lord in prayer and Bible study, then our fruitfulness is being swallowed up in bramble bushes.

Good ground

Only the last type of soil, the "good ground," which is soft and receptive to God's truths, free of hidden hurts or selfishness, and correctly prioritizes things in life, will ever bear the thirty-, sixty-, or hundredfold fruitfulness Jesus describes as possible in this parable.

Looking back, I was so blessed in my life. When I received my new heart from God, I was already surrounded by good people to help me pursue God with my whole heart from the first day of my Christian life. It was also so easy to contrast my former life with my new one—I had no legalistic religious thinking to hinder me from simply believing everything the Word of God had to say just as it was written. If I read, "Nothing is impossible with God," I simply believed it and put it into practice. If I failed, I simply went back to the Word to see if I had missed something and prayed for a better understanding. If I came to new hindrances in my heart or my life that I hadn't realized were there before, I dug them up, threw them away, and got back to nurturing the Word and the destiny I sensed in my heart. I wasn't perfect in all of this, but I was diligent in protecting my garden and caring for the seedlings of faith, truth, and purpose God had planted in my life. Over time they began to multiply and bear fruit that was a blessing not only to my life, but also to all the lives around me as well.

So, what kind of soil are you? And if you are not the good ground, what do you need to do be become good ground? God is calling you to thirty-, sixty-, and hundredfold fruitfulness, too. What are you going to do to bear it?

Part Four

Sow the Way
You Want to Go

Ten

Faithful in Little

Whoever can be trusted with very little can also be trusted with much, and whoever is dishonest with very little will also be dishonest with much. So if you have not been trustworthy in handling worldly wealth, who will trust you with true riches? And if you have not been trustworthy with someone else's property, who will give you property of your own?

—Luke 16:10–12, NIV

FOR MONTHS I thought about my pastor's question to me about planting a church, and eventually I knocked on his door with a question for him: "Do you still want to send me out?"

He didn't bat an eye, "Yes, of course. Where do you want to go?"

"Florida," I heard myself say before I had even considered the question.

"Fine," he said. "Just let me know what city, and then we can make all of the arrangements."

Now I would like to say I had fasted and prayed about this decision, or that God had just popped it into my spirit the instant my pastor had asked, but that would be a lie. I had just always wanted to go to Florida. When I was in school before I was arrested, I had thought I would go to college in Florida after I graduated. Somehow I just had it in me that I wanted to go to Florida, so when my pastor asked, that is what I answered.

I was still finishing some courses for my degree at this time, so I had access to the university library. I went there the next day and started studying about the state of Florida. Jacksonville was the largest city in square miles, Miami had the largest population, but I noticed that Orlando was the fastest growing. I did pray about it this time, specifically about going to Orlando, and God didn't say no, so that is where I decided we would plant a church.

The "Check" in Your Spirit

Some people wonder about taking things before the Lord like this, but Scripture does give us a precedent for it in the Book of Acts:

> Now when they [Paul and Silas] had gone through Phrygia and the region of Galatia, they were forbidden by the Holy Spirit to preach the word in Asia. After they had come to Mysia, they tried to go into Bithynia, but the Spirit did not permit them. So passing by Mysia, they came down to Troas. And a vision appeared to Paul in the night. A man of Macedonia stood and pleaded with him, saying, "Come over to Macedonia and help

us." Now after he had seen the vision, immediately we sought to go to Macedonia, concluding that the Lord had called us to preach the gospel to them.

—ACTS 16:6–10

I didn't have a vision, but the pattern here is that Paul and Silas started in one direction, but the Holy Spirit told them not to go that way. Then they tried a different direction, and the Holy Spirit again said no. Then, in exploring a third, the Holy Spirit gave them a confirmation that going to Macedonia was the right direction, so that's where they went.

In the Book of Colossians, Paul gives further explanation of this same idea. Here he advised:

Let the peace of God rule in your hearts.

—COLOSSIANS 3:15

This may seem a little obscure, but the point is that experiencing the peace of God inside is a guide. If you start to do something, and you feel like you have no *peace* about that decision—in other words, you feel really uncomfortable about the idea, and you know it is not fear or lack of confidence making you feel apprehensive—then that is probably not a direction that God wants you to go in. I think that is what happened with Paul and Silas as they started to head toward Bithynia; they just didn't have peace about it on the inside. A lot of believers call that a "check" in the Spirit. They decide to do something, and then wait to see how their heart feels about it. If they have peace about it, then it is a go; if they don't, then it is a *no*.

A lot of people mess this up because they want the vision so badly they overlook the check. These people are missing the supernatural because they are looking for the spectacular. God, however, prefers to work with us through our hearts and our daily relationship with Him. If we are willing to listen, then it is easier for Him to communicate with us.

I have also learned that the more directly God has to speak to you, the more trouble there is ahead. God spoke to Paul through a vision—and what awaited him and Silas in Macedonia? *Prison.* Part of the reason he and Silas could sing praises at the midnight hour while their feet were in shackles is that, because of the vision, Paul knew that they were in the center of God's will. It seems that the louder and the more directly God speaks to us, the rougher the seas are ahead. As for me, I would prefer this still, small voice in my heart to an audible voice any day of the week. So I keep my ear to my heart like those guys used to keep their ears to the ground in old westerns so that they knew how far away their enemies were.

Promotion Comes From the Lord

Over the years I have seen some important spiritual keys that moved me into destiny, which I didn't even realize were at work in my life at the time.

First of all, as I have said before, everything in the kingdom of God starts in seed form. For me, my ministry today started as a seed of destiny placed in my heart before I was born. Satan tried to destroy it, but God protected me. When I knelt on Douglas's basement floor and asked Jesus into my heart, that seed began to germinate. It led me to the university and then eventually into an executive staff position as the accountant of our church.

Yet in order to succeed, I had to follow a very important principle of the kingdom of heaven that works in just the opposite fashion than things operate in the kingdom of this earth. I had to follow the law of sowing and reaping. I had to *give* in order to *get*—and the more I gave, the more I got in return.

Now a lot of people only talk about this principle as it applies to money, but there is so much more we have to give. Giving starts as the basic principle of almost everything we receive. If we want to inherit eternal life, than we must *give* our lives to Jesus, accepting Him as our Lord and Savior. If we want to learn from an instructor in a university class, then we must respect him and give our attention and effort to do all the homework and reading that he assigns. The more effort and attention we give in class, the more we get in the form of knowledge and skills. On the job, the more we give of our efforts and apply ourselves to the task before us, the better we get at the job and the more likely we are to get a raise or promotion.

What we have to give generally comes in one of three forms: time, talent, or treasure (money). Most of us start by trading our time for treasure: we work so many hours a week for so many dollars an hour. As we grow in experience and training, our talents increase, and our time becomes more valuable. The only real difference between a fast-food worker who makes minimum wage and a lawyer who makes $750 an hour is their skills, talents, and what they know. If the minimum-wage worker is ever going to break through that minimum-wage ceiling, then that person is going to have to pick up skills and education that will take him or her into something better. Yet far too many in such positions choose to rob from their employers instead of sowing into them—they aren't looking to learn more or work harder, but instead they are looking for ways to slack off and not get caught. They are looking to find ways to cut corners and make their lives easier, but what they are doing instead is trapping themselves for the rest of their lives in the very work they are trying to avoid.

The story is often told of a hot August day when a group of men were working hard and sweating to replace railroad ties and adjust the track in some routine maintenance of a railway line. As they worked, an engine pulled up with a fancy caboose behind it that looked ready to go on a presidential tour of the nation. It was decked out with the company colors and looked cool and inviting. Out of it stepped a man dressed in a fancy business suit. He surveyed the work and then stopped as his eyes settled upon one of the workers. "John?" he called. "John Hayes, is that you?"

The man looked up. "Hey, Tom. Yes, it's me. Good to see you."

"Well, come on in for a minute to visit," the man called back from the caboose platform.

John laid down his shovel and walked up to Tom, who greeted him with a slap on the back. The two men disappeared inside the caboose.

Shortly afterward, John came out and returned to his shovel and his work. It wasn't long before the curiosity of his co-workers got the better of them, and one of them spoke up to ask, "John, isn't that Tom Miller, the president of the railroad?"

"Yep," John answered without looking up.

"Well, how do you know him?" another man asked.

At this, John dug the nose of his shovel into the ground and looked up. "We both started working for the railroad the exact same day over twenty years ago."

The other men looked at each other. Finally one of them spoke up to ask the obvious question: "John, if you both started the same day, how come Mr. Miller is the president of the railroad, and you're out here in the hot sun laying ties?"

"Well," John answered, regret filling his eyes as he leaned on his shovel, "twenty years ago Tom went to work for the railroad. I went to work for $1.20 an hour."

This story definitely illustrates something I have learned in my life: If all you are working for is a paycheck and to meet your own needs, that is all you will ever get. But if you are working to give your all to be a blessing to others, God will pass over a million others to draw you into your destiny.

Are You Paycheck-minded or Destiny-minded?

You see, that is what happened to me. Had I always had a paycheck mentality, I don't think I ever would have gone to the university and would still be working collections at that fitness club. I would have locked in on the fact that I didn't have the money for more schooling, only had a GED and not a regular diploma, and a hundred other reasons never to do anything but work for a paycheck that barely covered my expenses as it was.

Never Too Late

Key #12

When a farmer gathers his corn in the fall season, some of it is saved to plant in the spring season. Save your seed that will bring you another harvest season.

✠

Now may He who supplies seed to the sower, and bread for food, supply and multiply the seed you have sown and increase the fruits of your righteousness, while you are enriched in everything for all liberality, which causes thanksgiving through us to God.

—2 CORINTHIANS 9:10–11

Now, don't get me wrong, that was a pretty good job, and I was blessed to have it at the time, but God had put so much more than that in my heart. He wanted to take me out of my season of working there into a season of working as the accountant of the church, because in each season there was something I needed to learn and skills I needed to develop. Had I never excelled at either of those positions, I doubt very much that I would have had what it took to go on to the next season of my life and answer the call to plant a church in Orlando.

You see, wherever I have been, it was always my attitude that I would be the best I could be. Cream always rises to the top, and that is what I wanted to do. If I was going to be a collections representative, then I was going to be the best collections representative in the company. If I was going to be a student, then I would be the best student in the class. And if I was going to be a minister on the staff of a church, then I was going to be a faithful blessing to that church, our pastor, and everyone in its congregation.

You see, I wasn't just giving and then walking away expecting God to drop money on me from the sky in return; I was *investing*. I would sow my seed into the church, but then I would also pray over it to nourish it, apply my efforts to make sure it was fruitful, and speak the Word and truth over it to water it and see it grow. I wasn't just looking for what I could get out of it, but always what I could give to make things better. I made sacrifices when it was called for, holding the needs of others above my own as money ran short in salaries, but I had outside income to take care of my family, so it wasn't that bad. And oddly enough, the more I gave into the church, the more I grew and God blessed me, to the point where God saw I was ready for the next stage in coming into my destiny—calling me from the staff of the church in Baltimore to be the pastor of a church in Orlando. I had been faithful in that which was someone else's, and now God was going to give me something that would be my own.

132

All Destinies Start in Service to Others

Another thing I have seen along the way is that a lot of people focus in on the vision of their destiny, but they aren't interested in doing the work and putting in the effort to get them there. They are always looking for the easy way through or bossing others around and taking a leadership role they don't deserve. They come up in church asking if they can preach, but they aren't willing to serve anywhere in the church first. They want the glory of the leadership without any of the responsibility of letting God promote them into that place. They seem to have a great focus on their destinies, but they aren't willing to obey and serve their way into the position God is calling them toward.

The Bible is full of examples of this. Perhaps one of the most clear is that of Joseph. You see, Joseph had a dream from God that he would be a leader in his family. He was to be the chief prince of the princes of Israel, but Joseph was also spoiled and wanted to step into his dream right away. So when he was told by his father to deliver a message to his older brothers, he took it as a mandate to supervise and boss them around. In his arrogance, he did nothing but alienate the very people he was supposed to lead. What was he missing? A servant's heart. So when his brothers rose up to kill Joseph, God intervened through the voice of the oldest brother, Reuben, and instead of killing him, they sold him into Egypt where God could teach him to be a servant by having him live as a slave.

Moses did something very similar. He felt called to deliver Israel from the Egyptians, so when he saw a taskmaster beating a slave, he killed him. He thought he had to make God's calling on his life happen through the strength of his own hand. Instead of jump-starting his destiny, however, he was chased away as a murderer. So God took him to the backside of the desert where he learned to be a shepherd taking care of someone else's sheep. Then forty years later—once he had a servant's heart—God called him back to his original destiny of delivering God's people from slavery in Egypt.

Saul was a tall man and had the look of a king among all of his people, so when Israel demanded to be ruled by a king, God had him anointed to rule. However, the position and the calling went to his head, and he disobeyed God's direct instructions to him. God needed another to rule, so this time He looked for someone with a servant's heart—the youngest in his family who had the lowest position of caring for the sheep in the hills. In this young boy, David, God found the king He was really looking for, a man after His own heart.

Jesus said it best:

> You know that those who are considered rulers over the Gentiles lord it over them, and their great ones exercise authority over them. Yet it shall not be so among you; but whoever desires to become great among you shall be your servant. And whoever of you desires to be first shall be slave of all. For even the Son of Man did not come to be served, but to serve, and to give His life a ransom for many.
>
> —MARK 10:42–45

Do you want God to promote you into your destiny and call others to serve you in it? Then you need to find another person's destiny that you can serve faithfully and into which you can sow your time, talent, and treasure so that God can build you up into what He needs you to be. You need to pray for it, speak the Word and truth over it, and work to see it prosper and flourish, whether it is a ministry, a job, your family, or something you are volunteering your time for. And when you do so faithfully, God will notice and call you into what He has wanted to give you since before you were born. If you are faithful over little, He will promote you into bigger things.

Eleven

Don't Despise
the Wilderness

Truly, truly, I say to you, unless a grain of
wheat falls into the earth and dies, it remains
alone; but if it dies, it bears much fruit.
—*John 12:24,* ESV

S OME WEEKS LATER, our pastor stood before the congregation, as he had always done when sending out a new church
plant, and said, "Pastor Zach is going out to plant a church in
Orlando, Florida. Who wants to go with him?" Somewhere around
forty people raised their hands, and the die was cast. We were leaving Baltimore for the first time in my life.

Around this time I made two exploratory trips to Orlando to
spy out the land. Though I had no idea what to do in the natural,

I listened and prayed all the harder in the Spirit to get God's guidance. The most important issue was where God wanted us to plant the church, and then from there we would find a home that was nearby. We had no family or friends in the area, so I knew nothing about the area except for what I had researched about it in Baltimore. The first trip down, I had done on my own, but on the second trip, I brought my family.

On this second trip while Riva and the kids were taking in the sights, I got into the car and just started driving. Since I still didn't know the area, it wasn't long before I got lost, or at least I thought I was lost! Somehow in the process of driving around looking for a main road so that I could figure out where I was, I came to the intersection of Hiawassee and Silver Star Road, which is in northwest Orlando about fifteen to twenty miles from the hotel where we were staying. As I stopped at the light, I heard the Holy Spirit say, "Right here. Right here is where you'll begin." I marked the intersection on my map so I would remember it.

Later I found out that the area was called Pine Hills, but it had the nickname of "Crime Hills" as it had a negative stigma due to some violence and drug activity that had been in the papers. Though its reputation has changed in recent years, local residents still get angry if they hear that name. I determined that as soon as we moved I would start looking for a building near that intersection to plant the church.

When it finally came time to move, four people came with us. To get started, we rented a room in a downtown hotel in Orlando that was about fifteen minutes from the Pine Hills area, and our first service for New Destiny Christian Center was held there in June of 1996. For the next two or three months we stayed there, and I aggressively looked for a building in Pine Hills, but it wasn't as easy as I thought it would be. Nothing seemed to be available. No doors were opening. It seemed like no one was really interested in having a new church in that area, or else the lease amounts were just too high for a startup church such as ours, especially considering that I was trying to be a full-time pastor right from the start.

Meanwhile in the hotel, not much happened as far as growth. A few stragglers came by from time to time, but no one really stayed. We began to wonder if we had missed something.

However, after two months of looking, I found an empty location that could work in a very depressed shopping center at the intersection of Silver Star and Pine Hills Road. We soon signed a two-year lease on a 3,400-square-foot storefront and held our first service in the new location on the fourth Sunday of August 1996. It was a raggedy building that was infested with cockroaches, but it was there that God met us and the church began to grow. At the first service twenty-seven people showed up, and we thought we were experiencing revival. However, things soon slowed down again and times grew more desperate.

As things were working out, there wasn't enough money coming in for either Riva or I to take a salary, but we never stopped working to build it up—everything was "church, church, church," with little time to do anything else. When we left, our home congregation in Baltimore had promised support of $1,000 a week for the first year, but that was reduced to $500 a week after eight weeks, and then stopped completely about three months later—right after we had moved into the storefront. Almost from the beginning we were facing financial difficulties both for the church and for us personally. Riva soon got a job, but we still had difficulties just keeping the lights on and the water running. Plus we had two children at home who were both in diapers.

For the next two years we poured our life into the church and fell slowly into debt. We lived paycheck to paycheck, hand to mouth. At the end of our money there was always more month left over, so we had to borrow and were slowly sinking under a mountain owed to creditors. Yet we still diligently applied ourselves to what God had put in our hearts, giving our time, talents, and tithe to the church even though it meant other expenses weren't being met.

Expect the Tests

As we already discussed in a previous chapter, greatness always starts in darkness. Seeds grow in darkness, because when a seed is planted into the ground, for a season the seed is in darkness before it sends its leaves to the surface in search of light. Nobody likes the dark period, but it's in the dark period the power is released for you to spring forth. When the seed is underneath the soil, something happens. You could leave the seed on top of the soil, and nothing would ever happen except that it would be eaten by a bird or other animal. The seed fares poorly on the top of the ground. It has to get inside of the soil for it to really take root, and deep inside the soil is a dark, dark place.

On the way to anything worth doing, there will be times of darkness. In the Bible these often come in the wilderness. These are times when your resolve, commitment, maturity, and discipline are tested before you can go on to the next period of fruitfulness in your life.

Not even Jesus escaped this. Before His ministry began, the Bible tells us:

> Then Jesus, being filled with the Holy Spirit, returned from the Jordan and was led by the Spirit into the wilderness, being tempted for forty days by the devil. And in those days He ate nothing, and afterward, when they had ended, He was hungry.... Now when the devil had ended every temptation, he departed from Him until an opportune time. Then Jesus returned in the power of the Spirit to Galilee, and news of Him

138

went out through all the surrounding region. And He taught
in their synagogues, being glorified by all.

—LUKE 4:1–2, 13–15

It is good to get this story into the context of Jesus' life on the
earth. In Luke chapter 3, Jesus was baptized in the Jordan River by
John. The Bible tells us that after Jesus was baptized, "the Holy Spirit
descended in bodily form like a dove upon Him, and a voice came
from heaven which said, 'You are My beloved Son; in You I am well
pleased'" (Luke 3:22). That must have been something. Everyone
standing there saw Jesus filled with the Holy Spirit and heard God
speak His approval over Him (even if some of them didn't understand it because of their hard-heartedness). Jesus was ready to step
right into His ministry with power, right? Wrong. Instead of being
led out to preach, the Spirit of God led Him into the wilderness.

There, for forty days and forty nights, Jesus prayed and fasted.
We have no record in the Scriptures of God ever speaking to Him
during this time; in fact, the only person who showed up was the
devil! The Bible tells us that Jesus was tired and hungry, and that
was when Satan came to try to trip Him up.

The wilderness is not a fun place. It is the place where you
wander looking for the right direction and wonder what is happening with God. Did you do something to offend Him? Has He
abandoned you? Or is He just busy with more important people?
Did you really hear correctly in the first place? Is there someplace
else you should be where you could better hear His voice?

The wilderness is a place where you are hungry—and in those
early years in Orlando we were hungry. We wanted to see God
move and were growing hungrier by the day for our financial situation to straighten out. We were also tired from working long hours
and from working so hard for such small results. It was also a place
where hearing from God was not as it had been before. We would

pray for direction and guidance, and it seemed like God was ignoring us. And, just as it had happened with Jesus, after days of fasting and calling on God, the devil was the only one who showed up.

Doubts began to nag at us. We knew the way things were going was not according to the promises in Scripture. We were not living the abundant life Jesus said He had come to bring, nor were we prospering and in health, even as our souls prospered. We wondered if we had missed God in coming to Orlando, or if we had done something wrong to chase Him away. We wondered if we should give it up and go find jobs somewhere else, or if we weren't doing enough to make everything work. We began to doubt what we were doing. We questioned whether we had what it took to succeed and wondered if it was really worth the struggle and hardships.

We really had no idea what to do, so we just went back to the last thing we had heard from God—to go to Orlando and plant a church—and we stuck with that. In the end, that turned out to have been the right thing to do. Just as it had been for Jesus, we discovered that the wilderness was a testing and training place to see if we were ready to handle more power and responsibility from God.

Notice that the Scriptures tell us that when Jesus' time of testing was over, "Jesus returned in the power of the Spirit to Galilee." He had new power in His words, and His fame spread instantly— God's favor was also upon Him as it never had been before while He was on the earth. Jesus' faithfulness and continued commitment in the wilderness won Him access to more of God's miracle-working power as He resisted and defeated the devil with the Word of God. If we can show the same faithfulness and commitment through our wilderness times, then it will open up new power and authority in our walk as well as accomplish the destiny God has put within us.

Jesus is ever our pattern. Do we want to walk in more power? Do we want to know the will of God and speak nothing but what God tells us to say? Then we need to be in prayer constantly and daily just as Jesus was, and we need to know the Word of God until it oozes out of every pore. That way, when we are tempted, we respond with God's Word; when we are in crisis, we respond with God's Word; when we are stressed, we respond with God's Word; and regardless of what happens, the Word of God is the first thing that comes to our minds and to our mouths.

Now, I have been led into the wilderness because of my own sin, and I have been led into the wilderness because the Spirit of God led me there. When sin leads you into the wilderness, it is because you are not looking to God and His Word for direction. When you are in there because of sin, it is heavy and burdensome, and you don't know how you're going to get out. I don't know about you, but I don't want to be led into the wilderness because of sin. I'd rather that God lead me to the wilderness. And then, when the test comes, I want to pass it and get to the next level.

When you are led by the Spirit into the wilderness as Jesus was, then it is a test to prepare you for promotion. It is a temporary holding place to make sure you can handle the power and responsibility that God is about to release upon your life. Do you have the commitment and resolve to see it through despite persecution or hardships? Do you have the discipline not to get caught up with the cares of this world, the deceitfulness of riches, or lusts for other things and to keep your priorities straight? Do you have the maturity to press on with what God has already put in your heart and not waver because you haven't had a "fresh word" from Him lately? Or are you so hungry for God's voice that you will push to hear any voice, regardless of whether it agrees with the Bible or not? Are you patient enough to stick with His Word no matter what?

We can only pass the wilderness tests if we stick to God's Word and continue to seek intimacy with Him through the entire experience. How you handle the wilderness determines the capacity of what you can receive from God. It is just like in school: if you pass the final exam, then that proves you are ready to go on to the next level.

How Much Can God Trust You?

You see, when God tests us in wilderness times, He is trying to determine two things:

1. Can He trust us if He gives us more wealth, responsibility, or power to do what He has called us to do?

2. Would giving us more wealth, responsibility, or power be a blessing to us, or would it be a curse?

Though this applies in several areas, perhaps it is most easily seen with money.

There was a reason that Jesus spoke about money more than almost any other topic besides the kingdom of God: He knew that money would be one of the biggest stumbling blocks Christians would ever face. He knew that it could become more intoxicating than alcohol and more addictive than cocaine. He knew that there were only two relationships a person can have with money: either it would be our master, or we would learn to master it. As Jesus said:

> No servant can serve two masters. Either he will hate the one and love the other, or he will be devoted to the one and despise the other. You cannot serve both God and Money.
> —LUKE 16:13, NIV

Just as it was in Jesus' day, though probably more today than any other time in the history of the world, people commonly have two ways of getting what they want: (1) they can exercise hard work and self-discipline, or (2) they can borrow from their futures to buy what they want today. The first is to put your resources to work for you to accomplish your goals; the second is to be subject to your wants and desires and serve the lenders who advanced you the money to get those things.

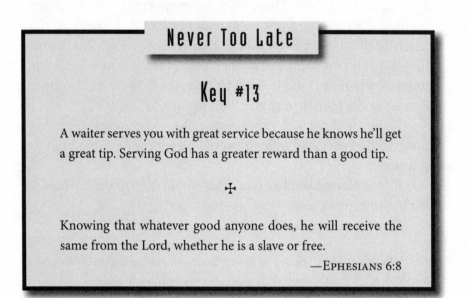

Never Too Late

Key #13

A waiter serves you with great service because he knows he'll get a great tip. Serving God has a greater reward than a good tip.

✚

Knowing that whatever good anyone does, he will receive the same from the Lord, whether he is a slave or free.

—EPHESIANS 6:8

A lot of us wish that God would dump big checks on us like we have heard He does on ministers who preach to us about prosperity, but the truth of the matter is that if He did that for many of us, we would be worse off in a few months than we are today. If you cannot master your money when you have just a little of it, it is like a house with weak and leaky plumbing. As long as you don't run too much water through it, there is only a small puddle in the basement that isn't too bad, but if you turn the water up to full pressure, then the whole system is liable to burst and flood the basement!

Every year or so, newspapers seem to run an article about past lottery winners who are worse off today than they were before they won all of those millions. Before, they had run-down cars that they didn't really take care of, credit cards maxed out, bills unpaid, and so forth. After they won all that money, they have new things all over that are just as uncared for and on the way to falling apart as their old cars were—they have twice the credit cards that are maxed out, and their bills are just as unpaid because they spent all the money fulfilling their every want and desire with no self-discipline. They didn't invest a dime of it, they didn't turn it into a profitable business, and they chose to live a few months in the high life rather than using the money to secure their futures.

Many of them say they wished they had never seen that money. What they had thought would be a blessing turned out to be a curse.

If God blessed you like that, what would it do to you? Would it be a blessing, or a curse?

This is why Jesus said:

> Whoever can be trusted with very little can also be trusted with much, and whoever is dishonest with very little will also be dishonest with much. So if you have not been trustworthy in handling worldly wealth, who will trust you with true riches?
>
> —LUKE 16:10–11, NIV

What are true riches? A stronger walk with God and hearing His voice more clearly; people who will trust you and invest in your destiny; the fruit of the Spirit; the gifts of the Spirit; peace in your home; a successful marriage that lasts a lifetime; kids who want to come home for Thanksgiving with their families and aren't trying to sue you to pay for their psychiatric bills because you neglected them when they were children; and any number of other blessings that will both bring you joy and equip you to better fulfill all that God has put in your heart to do. Certainly cars, houses, trust funds, and

the like can come with those things, but if that is all you are
are really missing it. You will get the riches and a life of
heartache with it just as so many millionaires experience t

True riches come through the methods, not the rest
riches come from hearing from God through His Word ar
and obeying His voice. Anything less is a formula for dis
ment.

If you knew your kid was drinking and taking drug
you buy him a new car so that he could go to parties on his
the weekends? Of course not; it would be like ramming hir
brick wall yourself because you know that is where he wo
up. In the same way, God knows better than to dump ri
you if they will only drive you further from Him and into a
bondage to your bill collectors. Get real! God isn't stupid.

But if your daughter is enrolled in college and needs a
get there and to work, blessing her with a car is reasonable. I
going to fill it with people to bring to church every Sunday,
be all the easier to bless her in this way.

When the Israelites were delivered from Egypt, they hac
through the wilderness to get to the Promised Land. God's
nal plan was that they would only spend a week or so there t
He brought them into the land "flowing with milk and honey
their disobedience turned that two-week vacation into forty
of traveling in circles!

Too many Christians are trying to go around the wilder
They want to get the blessings without obeying God or wor
to apply His Word to their hearts and building the character,
discipline, and wisdom needed so that God's blessings will be bl
ings not only to them, but also to everyone their lives touch.
many want to climb under and go over or navigate around
wilderness, but there must be a wilderness experience for there

be an elevation experience. God can't trust you with more until you have been tried and tested to increase your capacity to handle it.

Why are you fighting going into the wilderness experience when that is the only way you are going to move to the next level? You want better, you want bigger, you want more, you're praying for more, you're crying for more, but you don't want to go through the test to get more! Don't you know for every new level there is a test you have to pass?

Can God trust you with more? If so, expect—and pass—the wilderness tests, because what is on the other side is worth it.

As David said in Psalm 23:4 (KJV), "Yea, though I walk through the valley of the shadow of death, I will fear no evil: for thou art with me." He knew in his darkest hour that what was on the other side of the valley was worth the journey, and that God had not forsaken him, but was testing him to increase his capacity for blessing.

God is looking for more people after His own heart just like David who will stay the course through the storms. Are you one of them?

Twelve

You Will Reap
What You Sow

Give, and it will be given to you: good
measure, pressed down, shaken together,
and running over will be put into your
bosom. For with the same measure that you
use, it will be measured back to you.

—*Luke 6:38*

IN THE SPRING of 1997, we were completely on our own and continuing to struggle. I had lots of time to pray and study the Word, so I used it and did everything I could think of to understand what God wanted us to do next.

Sometime around March of that year I attended a conference where I met Pastors Randy and Paula White, who had a thriving church in Tampa Bay. In passing somewhere, he had asked me to come to his church in Tampa and attend one of his conferences, so I did. During this time we had a chance to sit down and see if he could help me with what was happening—or not happening as it were—in Orlando.

After listening to me explain some of the details, he turned to me and pointedly asked, "What makes your church different from all the other churches on your block? What makes your church stand out?"

I honestly couldn't answer him. As I thought about it, I thought, *OK, what does make us stand out? What do we stand for? We're just another church teaching the Bible; why would anyone notice us as being different?*

Then he asked me another question. "What are you doing to sow into your community?"

I had to again answer, "I don't know. We're just teaching the Word."

He looked at me for a moment, and then asked another question. "If you are not sowing anything into your community, how do you expect to reap any kind of a harvest of church members from it?"

On that, he had me. All this time in lack, I had been focused on receiving, but in that moment I realized that we needed to change our focus from being a receiving church to a giving church! I determined that we would be an outreach church and not a "build it and they will come" church.

In the following weeks, I learned about every outreach program the Whites had at their church, and I made plans to put them into action at our church, only on a scale more to the size of our present church. Miraculously as we began to organize, we found support for our efforts from all over, and groups such as Disney and Tupperware underwrote our efforts. We put up a tent in our parking lot and bussed people in from the homeless shelters for job fairs, medical and dental care, haircuts, meals, and whatever we could think of that they might need.

Then around that same time God spoke to me again very clearly and told me the craziest thing. He wanted me to start going on television. We only had about a hundred members in the church at the time, but He said to go on TV. It did fit with our outreach vision, though it would take virtually every penny we brought in to do it, but I had determined long before this to always obey God. So, somewhere around May or June of 1997, we started shooting for television and broadcasting locally. There I was, a pastor with a church of a hundred or so going on TV! It seemed crazy.

Then it wasn't long after that, Riva came home from work one day and told me she had a word from the Lord. I was so excited—until I heard what it was!

She told me God had told her to start sowing her entire salary check into the church. I thought at first she was nuts. I mean, we were barely scraping by. We were living off of boiled noodles and chicken pot pies that you could buy three for a dollar at the local supermarket. We had had our electricity cut off at one point. I mean, there I was, preaching, "Jesus is the light of the world," and I was living in the dark! I was preaching, "Jesus is the bread of life," and we had no bread in the cupboards. I am talking about making one cup of Kool-Aid at a time!

So when she said, "God told me to give my check to the church until He tells me to stop," I thought, *Shut your mouth! I know that ain't from God. That's just hunger pains weakening your mind! You're hallucinating!* The church wasn't running much more than fifty to eighty people on Sunday morning at that point, and all of its money was going to rent, utilities, TV, and other such expenses—so her salary was all the money we had to live on that we knew would be there from week to week.

But as we prayed about it, I felt God had actually told her to do this, so we came into agreement that we would continue to sow her check until God told her to stop. Each week after that, she wouldn't even cash her check, but just flipped it over, signed the back of it, put it in the envelope, and gave it to the church.

Now don't misunderstand—unless you get a direct word from God, I am not suggesting that you do this. Nor am I suggesting that you start a TV ministry with only a congregation of a hundred people. The key was not in the giving or outreaching alone, but in the obedience. Without these instructions being directly from God, they wouldn't have made any difference, and we would have been worse off for our foolishness and attempts to force the hand of God than we were before.

However, after about the eighth or ninth week of doing this, in October of that same year, a man showed up in our Sunday morning service whom I had never seen before. He wore a white T-shirt and jeans and sat all the way in the back. At the time, I didn't think anything of it—new people visited our services every once in a while—but after the service he came up to me and said, "Sir, I need to speak with you."

As I looked at him, I thought he might be a little off. I said, "Well, OK." I was trying to build a church, so I was open to helping anybody. I invited him back to my little makeshift, mismatched-furniture office expecting a counseling session. Instead, when we finally sat down, he said, "How much debt do you have?"

I thought, *Yep, he's crazy.* But there I was thinking too logical. I was a faith preacher, but I was thinking with my brain and not following the Spirit. So, since I thought he was nuts, I just made up a number "About $13,000," I said. As soon as I said it, he reached into his back pocket, pulled out his checkbook, wrote me a check for $13,000, handed it to me, and left.

You would have thought that I would have been jumping up and down celebrating and praising God, but I didn't. As soon as he left my office, I started crying on the inside, because I had a lot more debt than $13,000! I wasn't even believing what I was preaching! Here was a miracle staring me right in the face, and I had missed it because I was in disbelief!

You see, later I had the chance to hear the story of why he had come. He told me, "I was trying to sleep the night before, but every time I would roll over in my bed, I would hear 'Zachery Tims. Zachery Tims. Zachery Tims. Zachery Tims.' It happened again and again, no matter what I did. So in exasperation, I finally cried out, 'Who is Zachery Tims?' When I did, God told me who you were and where I could find you, so the next morning I showed up in your church. God sent me to pay off all of your personal debt in one day. So I just asked you how much you needed, wrote you a check, and left, because that is all God had told me to do."

There I was, believing with all my heart that we were obeying God and that He would break the power of debt off of our lives and start blessing the church, and then when someone walked in to do it, I didn't even believe it. I spent that afternoon torn between gratitude for what God had done and depression that He had showed up on our behalf, and I had missed the miracle He was trying to perform.

Now back in those days I used to have an evening service, not because it was needed—we never had more than ten to fifteen people who would show—but because I was so zealous I just had one anyway. Because of my missing God, I think my message was a little less heartfelt that night until about halfway through the same man walked in again and sat in almost exactly the same place in the back row. Again at the end of the service he came up and politely said, "I have to talk with you."

Obviously my response this time was very different. "Come on back! Can I get you a soda or juice or something else to drink?"

When we sat down in my office again, he simply said, "When I got home today, God told me I wasn't finished." So he wrote me another check for the rest of the money that we needed to pay off our debts. As it turned out, he would return again later, and sometime around January of 1998, he gave us enough money to buy our own television equipment so that we could shoot our own Sunday morning broadcasts and cut our videotaping expenses by more than half.

Soon after those first checks and as our outreach programs continued, things started to turn around. Our storefront could comfortably sit about two hundred fifty at one time, and by mid-1998 we had to go to two Sunday morning services a week and were running about three hundred fifty. For the next few years, the size of our church would continue to double every year. It was time to start looking for a bigger space.

God Blesses You So That You Can Change Your World

The blessings and power of God don't flow so that you can sit around and be fat and happy and contribute nothing to your world. Certainly there are people out there who receive financial and material blessings to such an extent that we can envy them, but we shouldn't. God isn't really looking to bless us just halfway. He wants us to have spiritual blessing too, and even more than material blessings that will only pass away after we are gone. The Bible tells us:

> The blessing of the LORD makes one rich,
> And He adds no sorrow with it.
>
> —PROVERBS 10:22

A lot of people spend their health to get their wealth, and then when they are older, they spend their wealth to get back their health. Others let their families fall apart as they build great companies or real estate empires, only to find out that their sons and daughters want nothing to do with them. And still others live like slaves to their creditors and from paycheck to paycheck because they can never break out of the cycle of debt. They never learn to make money their slave rather than allowing it to be their taskmaster.

Believe it or not, it is very possible to have everything you ever wanted and be completely miserable. But that is not God's plan. No matter how much you have, and no matter how spiritually strong you grow, if you don't find your purpose in life, none of it will really matter. That is why God gave us a destiny and a life's mission before we were ever born.

You have to understand that whatever God does, His intent is that you overflow in blessings. That you are so full of peace that people feel peaceful when you walk into a room. That you are so overflowing with joy that you constantly give joy to everyone around you. That's why He wants you to be joy*ful* and peace*ful* and money-*full*. He wants to bless you so much that you can be a blessing to every life with which you interact.

You see, God wants us overflowing with blessings in all areas. The key to that kind of blessing is wrapped up in hearing His voice, learning your personal destiny, and obeying His Word.

Get this: The closer you get, the more intimate your walk, and the stronger your worship, the more power you have available to you to realize your destiny and see it change your world! Why? Because the more He can trust you.

You don't just give anybody your checkbook, because you don't know what they might do with that authority. First you might give them a twenty-dollar bill and see what they do with that, and then maybe a hundred. The better I know and trust a person, the more likely I would be to trust them with my checkbook if I need to for some reason. In my church in Baltimore, my pastor came to trust me so much that he turned over managing his finances to me completely. I knew more about his money than he did! In fact, with some people you might even become so close that you not only let them care for your checkbook, but you also put their name on your checks! For instance, my checks don't just have "Zachery Tims" on them anymore, but they have "Zachery Tims or Riva Tims" on them because I know her so well that everything that I have I share with her. We are in the covenant of marriage together and have pledged everything we have to each other.

In the Bible, God was a covenant partner with those He could trust, too—men like Abraham, Isaac, Jacob, Joseph, Moses, and David. He is looking for more covenant partners like them today—people He can trust to share *His checkbook* with.

Some of you want power from God, but the only time you talk to God is on Sunday morning. You just have a casual relationship with God. It is a relationship of convenience. If you want to see God's blessings work in your life, then you have got to go deeper with God. Your relationship with Him has got to get more intimate. This kind of power is released to those that are willing to walk with Him every minute of every day.

I'm telling you that if you want to have an intimate walk with God and not be a casual Christian, then you are really going to have to work at it. You really need to get into the Word of God and apply that Word to your life. If you want the limitations to fall off—if you want to break free from sickness, if you want the power to break free from debt, the power to break free from marital distress, or the power to break free from any other problem you may face, then you are going to have to seek God for the answer through His Word, prayer, and times in His presence, and then obey His voice once you hear it.

154

How Blessing Comes

God wants to release power into your life that will change your situation or dilemma. He wants you to come out of the wilderness, to pass through the valley to get to the other side, to pass the test, trials, and persecutions so that He can stand strong on your behalf. His power is available to you today, but too many miss the blessing because they don't recognize it when it comes. They are looking for riches and expecting a big check to come in the mail or that they will win the lottery, but God really doesn't work that way. Like your destiny, blessings often come in seed form, because God wants to grow you up through the process of you taking the seed of blessing and bringing it to fruition.

Never Too Late

Key #14

A successful entrepreneur gains more wealth because he knows the principle of investing. When you invest in the work of God, you are making a deposit in the bank of heaven. When you need a withdrawal, it will be there.

✠

Honor the LORD with your possessions,
And with the firstfruits of all your increase;
So your barns will be filled with plenty,
And your vats will overflow with new wine.

—PROVERBS 3:9–10

The Bible tells us:

> You shall remember the LORD your God, for it is He who gives
> you power to get wealth, that He may establish His covenant
> which He swore to your fathers, as it is this day.
>
> —DEUTERONOMY 8:18

What is this saying exactly? That God gives us the power to get
wealth so that His kingdom may be established on the earth—so
that we will create a place or an atmosphere in which His covenant
promises can flow as freely as if we were standing before His throne
in heaven. What is a kingdom, anyway? It is a place where the will
of the king is the law of the land. If we live in a place where God's
healing power is not available to everyone, where His promises for
prosperity, joy, and peace do not happen in the lives of His people,
where the devil seems to have more influence in our lives than God
does, then we are not yet living in God's kingdom, because the Bible
tells us:

> The kingdom of God is…righteousness and peace and joy in
> the Holy Spirit.
>
> —ROMANS 14:17

But if God is actively trying to get us this kingdom, and we are
actively trying to live in it, why isn't it manifesting more? I think
one of the big problems is that too many of us are looking for the
wrong kinds of blessings and aren't willing to take the seeds, plant
them, and nurture them to the point that they yield enough fruit of
the kingdom to share with all around us.

Again, wealth is not just money. Wealth is really the ability
to get whatever we need to get the job done. Certainly money can
be a help in that. If we have a huge pile of money, then we can hire
people to work for us, buy needed materials, hire consultants who

are experts in getting done what we want to get done, advertise to gain public support, or in one way or another trade that money for accomplishing almost any task before us. Money can literally move mountains.

But then, so can faith, and that is where I think we miss what true wealth really is.

Using money to do the work is easier than using faith and requires no growth or spiritual fruitfulness for us in the process. Faith, however, does. If we have money, then we don't have to have character to influence others. We don't really need righteousness. We don't have to pray. We don't have to walk intimately with God. We can pretty much do whatever we want just by waving $100 bills around, but then live in spiritual poverty.

God is more interested in fellowshiping with us, so He rarely dumps bags of money on us unless He is sure it won't make any difference to how we walk with Him. He wants to work through every step of the journey with us, show us the way, and watch our joy at the accomplishment of His promises.

This is why those of you who are waiting for money to fall out of heaven will be waiting until you die. It's not going to happen. Money does not fall from a tree or from heaven on those God loves. Instead it comes in the form of an uncommon idea or a unique command that we will have to work to make grow into a blessing.

Let's say, for instance, God gives you the idea to create a community center that can teach life skills to adolescents in your area. If you have a wad of cash, you could build a building, name it after yourself, hire a staff, and go to work. If you had enough money, you could even pay kids to come, but what would you really have? Chances are, because no one else really had to invest in the project, it would only last as long as your money did.

But let's say instead all you had was the idea. First thing you would need to do is pray and seek God for more details to the vision—something you would have to continue to do throughout the entire project. Then you would have to take that vision and share it with others and get them seeking God to see what their part was in making this vision a reality. You would have to study so that you could write the grants that could supply you with money to get started. You would have to win the hearts of people in the community so that you could get space in a building somewhere to hold your classes. You would have to find ways to publicize it on a tight budget. You would have to be disciplined in everything you did. You would have to keep your promises, build a reputation so that others would trust you, develop a curriculum built on truths that would transform lives, and invest in one kid at a time. You would have to stick to it through the tough wilderness times when it looked like there was no hope of your dream ever happening. You would have to exercise wisdom, patience, kindness, integrity, humility, self-control, character, and so many other qualities that honor God.

In the end, what you have may look just the same on the outside as the community center built by the person with a pile of cash, but yours will last because the riches you used to build it also enriched all those whose lives your dream touched. Yes, you will need some money along the way too, but what you build with it will be very different. In the first example, the people working are working for the paycheck; in the second, the paycheck is liberating the workers to pursue the dream. On the outside it may look the same, but there is all the difference in the world on the inside.

Too often, we see manifestations of material possessions, but that is not where the power is. The power is in the connection to God, living in His ways, and in obedience to His instructions. The minute you start obeying the instructions, the materials needed to accomplish the dream will start coming toward you.

Too many look at the blessings and focus on getting them, but they miss the real power that is in the dream and the destiny. Power to get wealth is locked into a command that makes a demand on your faith, not on money falling from heaven. The easy road is seldom God's way.

The road to your destiny is not through the acquisition of material blessings, but material blessings will come by pursuing your destiny. Don't get the two confused. While the end may look the same on the outside, the differences inside are as far apart as heaven and hell. True riches spring from hearing and obeying God's voice; realizing your destiny is completely wrapped up in pursuing Him.

Part Five

Live From the
Fruit of Your Gifts;
Let God Establish
Your Calling

Thirteen

Everything You Set
Your Hand To

The LORD will command the blessing on
you in your storehouses and in all to which
you set your hand, and He will bless you in
the land which the LORD your God is giving
you.

—*Deuteronomy 28:8*

I N AUGUST OF 1998, we signed a one-year extension for the
storefront and started earnestly seeking our own building, even
though we had no money for one. However, I knew in my heart
we would not sign another yearly lease in that location. It was time
we owned something of our own. It was time for the church to move
to another level, so we started looking again.

After a false start and a setback on a building on Lee Road, we
returned to look at an old Baptist church on Powers Drive that was

only about three minutes from our storefront. The first time I had seen it, I felt a strong *no* inside of me, but upon the return some months later, it was as if I had never been in the building before. Again I heard God say, "Right here. This is the building I want you to buy." It was on fourteen acres, with fifty-four thousand square feet that was mostly classrooms. The sanctuary, which comfortably sat six hundred to seven hundred, was expandable, and there was a separate building that housed a gymnasium. As far as I was concerned, it was perfect and would meet our needs for several years to come.

So, in May or June of 1999, we signed a contract to buy this building, with the stipulation that we have the down payment of $300,000 before we took possession of it in September. At the time, we had only $70,000 in the building fund. So in the next three months we would have to raise more three times that much to be able to close on it.

As it happened, God directed us to have a weeklong revival in July, and despite the summer heat, we filled our little storefront to the brim, running services of as many as three hundred. We brought in a guest speaker, and the church was packed out every night. In that one week, we also brought in about $125,000 for our new building. By the grace of God, in the remaining months the rest came in, and we were set for our first service in the new building by the last Sunday of August 1999.

Because of the limitations of our storefront, I had never preached to more than three hundred people at any one time in Orlando, but during our first service in the Powers Drive building, nearly a thousand people showed up. The sanctuary was full. We had folding chairs set up, people were standing along the walls, and then we also lined up folding chairs in the foyer. We had only just moved in, and we were already overflowing. God was moving, and the church was doubling again.

In November, just two months later, I was driving to work on a Monday, and as I came to an intersection, the Holy Spirit spoke to my heart, "Make a left turn." Discerning that it was in fact the Holy Spirit, I obeyed. A mile up the road, I heard, "Make another left turn." Again, I obeyed, this time looking at the street sign to see where I was so I wouldn't get lost. I was turning onto McCormick Road. It was an area I had never been in before. A little way down this road, I saw a sign on a huge corner lot that read, "Faith World is coming." Then I again heard the Holy Spirit who said, "Park right here." When I did, all I felt led to do was pray, so I did. Some time later I felt a release, so I continued on to work as if it had never happened.

On my way to work the next morning, the same thing happened again. Then on Wednesday, the third day, it happened again. This time after praying, however, I heard the Holy Spirit say, "This land is yours."

I knew He meant it was for the church. All I could do was blurt out, "We just bought a church! We just moved not even sixty days ago. We don't have any money! I don't know how much it costs, but even if it were only a dollar, we don't have that! Everything is wrapped up in our new building!"

But the Holy Spirit just repeated, "*This* is your land."

When Thursday morning came, I heard the same thing and ended up under the same sign. Friday proved to be the same, but again the Holy Spirit added something new: "I want you to call about this land." It was a Friday. I was tired of fighting, so when I got to the office I found a number for Faith World and called, figuring I wouldn't get an answer. As I expected, I left a voice message, and I figured I was finally free. Only just a few hours later I got a call back from Faith World. It was their administrator, who said, "Pastor Clint wants to meet with you on Monday morning."

165

So I went to meet with Pastor Clint Brown that Monday. It was a beautiful building, and I was led into a conference room to await him. A few minutes later, the pastor walked in. He had a set of blueprints in his hand, and he tossed them on the table and said, "I've been waiting for some preacher to be bold enough to call me about that land." My jaw must have hit the table!

Then he pointed at the blueprints, "We have drawings, we have the approvals, we have everything in place to build there, but we changed our mind and bought another building instead. Do you want it?"

This time my jaw must have hit the floor. I couldn't believe it! All I could think to do was blurt out, "Um, how much do you want for it?"

"Well," he said, "we paid three hundred and something thousand for it. I will sell it to you for what we paid for it." It was twenty-one acres of land. That was an incredible deal, but what was I going to do? We were just able to keep up with the loan we had on the new building we just purchased, and I knew no banker in his right mind would loan us money for new land with that note outstanding. So that is what I told him. Pastor Clint just responded that they would carry the note until we could get proper financing. Again, I couldn't believe it. So, within a few weeks time we worked out the paperwork and acquired the property. We ended up starting construction on that building in May 2001, and that land is where our main church sanctuary is today.

When God Is Ready to Move, You Need to Be Ready, Too!

The changing of the seasons of our lives can be times of tremendous and rapid adjustment. For any season or place that we are in, there is a grace to be there. This is why people who are called to be ministers in tough inner-city areas, a war-torn province, or remote mountain villages where there is no running water or electricity can flourish in these areas while others would flounder. God gives them a special strength to be in that difficult place and thrive while everyone else is suffering and hopeless. But when that grace starts to move, we need to be ready to move with it, or else we can fall behind and miss the opportunities that God has for us.

This happened to Isaac in the land of the Philistines:

> There was a famine in the land, besides the first famine that was in the days of Abraham. And Isaac went to Abimelech king of the Philistines, in Gerar. Then the LORD appeared to him and said: "Do not go down to Egypt; live in the land of which I shall tell you. Dwell in this land, and I will be with you and bless you; for to you and your descendants I give all these lands, and I will perform the oath which I swore to Abraham your father. And I will make your descendants multiply as the stars of heaven; I will give to your descendants all these lands; and in your seed all the nations of the earth shall be blessed; because Abraham obeyed My voice and kept My charge, My commandments, My statutes, and My laws." So Isaac dwelt in Gerar.
>
> —GENESIS 26:1–6

As we go further into this story, we see that Isaac not only obeyed and stayed in this place of dead, dry ground, but he also sowed into it and expected a crop when no one around him was growing anything.

> Then Isaac sowed in that land, and reaped in the same year a hundredfold; and the LORD blessed him.
>
> —GENESIS 26:12

Normally when finances get tight, the natural thing to do is to hold on tighter to what we have. But when things get tight, those who are kingdom-minded start letting more things go. They give more to their church and more to local charities, they work harder at their jobs, they study harder to gain wisdom and knowledge to see them through, and they work harder to bear spiritual fruit for all around them to see. Even when they run out of money to give away, they start giving away clothes, shoes, furniture, food, or whatever isn't nailed down.

For us, when we were in a tight place in Orlando, we knew we needed to reap a harvest to make things change. You can't reap a harvest unless you are willing to sow. Our changes came when we learned to change our church from just another church into a giving church, and though we had no money to give, we did have time and organizational talent. We also knew how to get a prayer through to open up heaven for those around us. A lot of times, if you work with what you do have, the rest will fall into place; thus, as we started to share our vision of outreach ministries to help the needy and homeless people in our communities, corporate sponsors joined us and helped to support the cost. The church family supplied the manpower, the prayer power, and the love necessary to make our outreaches work.

Why? Because the more we give—and the more of ourselves we make available for God to use—the more His light will shine! The key is to give God the little that you have so that He has something to multiply!

We can see this principle at work in the life of Isaac. He obeyed God's voice to stay in Gerar, and he sowed in a land of famine—and he received a hundredfold return in that same year! God doesn't need a lot of time to turn things around, which we discovered at our church. Just a few years after we changed into a giving church, God took us from about a hundred members to roughly a thousand, and we continued to multiply supernaturally over the next few years. Just like with a seed that is planted in the ground and watered, for a while nothing seems to happen, and then before you know it, the seed sprouts fruit and is produced.

Look what happened to Isaac as a result of his obedience:

> The man began to prosper, and continued prospering until he became very prosperous; for he had possessions of flocks and possessions of herds and a great number of servants. So the Philistines envied him. Now the Philistines had stopped up all the wells which his father's servants had dug in the days of Abraham his father, and they had filled them with earth. And Abimelech said to Isaac, "Go away from us, for you are much mightier than we." Then Isaac departed from there and pitched his tent in the Valley of Gerar, and dwelt there.
> —Genesis 26:13–17

In the midst of a famine in the land, God blessed him. He went from "prospering," to "continuing to prosper," to "becoming very prosperous." The King James Version calls these three levels "waxing great," "moving forward," and becoming "very great." These are three levels that God wants to work in our lives as we work the principle of giving.

Get Out of Personal Debt

To me, "waxing great" is the level where God starts to prosper you enough to pay off your debts. How do I know that "waxing great" is dealing with your debt? Because a household can't move forward with a bunch of debt! If you have debt—especially bad debt like credit card debt or debt on things that depreciate the minute you take them out of the store or drive them off the lot—then you are not beginning to prosper yet. Financial prosperity begins when you can pay cash for whatever you want. If you are going to prosper financially God's way, the first thing that God is going to do is get you out of debt.

Look at what the Bible says again about the commanded blessing:

> The LORD will command the blessing on you in your store-houses and in all to which you set your hand, and He will bless you in the land which the LORD your God is giving you.
> —DEUTERONOMY 28:8

What is your storehouse? It was the seed farmers saved to live off of for the next year, to sow the next year, and to keep in reserve in case the next year's crop failed. If you don't have extra money or other investments in the bank, then you don't have a storehouse! How is God going to bless your storehouses if you don't have any?

This is the principle God planted in us in October 1997 after we had changed our vision for outreaches to become a giving church. He got us out of debt. The first thing He did was provide the means for us to be able to pay off our debt. As a result, we began to see our church and community that we had been sowing into start to experience increase and to prosper as well.

The season of getting out of debt will lead to the season of "moving forward," but God doesn't want us to stop and get comfortable there. He wants us to push on to becoming so "very great" that the world looks at us and is jealous! He wants us to be just like Isaac, who, in a season of famine, sowed and reaped a hundredfold blessings and became so great that the Philistines envied him.

What would it be like if rappers and movie stars started envying the church? What would it be like if NFL, NBA, and MLB players started longing for what the people sitting in the pews had because it was so much more real, true, and satisfying?

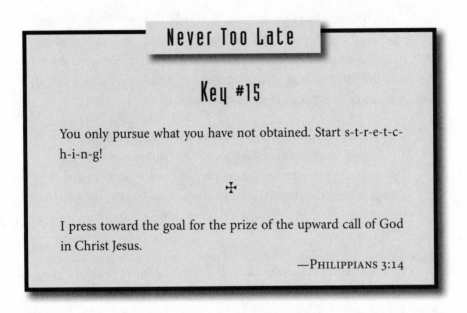

Never Too Late

Key #15

You only pursue what you have not obtained. Start s-t-r-e-t-c-h-i-n-g!

☩

I press toward the goal for the prize of the upward call of God in Christ Jesus.

—PHILIPPIANS 3:14

There is a place in the Bible where the world envies the church rather than the church envying the world. That is the way it is supposed to be. We are supposed to be so submitted to God, so humble in God, so committed to God, and so in tune with His Spirit that blessings will start overtaking our lives to such an extent that the world will become jealous of what God is doing for us. Deuteronomy 28:12 says:

> Now it shall come to pass, if you diligently obey the voice of the LORD your God, to observe carefully all His commandments which I command you today, that the LORD your God will set you high above all nations of the earth. And all these

blessings shall come upon you and overtake you, because you obey the voice of the LORD your God.

The Philistines so envied Isaac that they chased him away from the good land and forced him into the lowlands, probably pushing him from the edge of the famine into the heart of it. He was no longer near the city; he was now in the valley, the low point of Gerar. But Isaac didn't despair. He just started over.

And Isaac dug again the wells of water which they had dug in the days of Abraham his father, for the Philistines had stopped them up after the death of Abraham. He called them by the names which his father had called them. Also Isaac's servants dug in the valley, and found a well of running water there.

—GENESIS 26:18–19

It was a famine, a drought, and yet in the most desolate place the Philistines could drive Isaac to, he had his servants dig, and they found water. It's like old Jed Clampett of the 1960s' sitcom *The Beverly Hillbillies*—he's just out hunting rabbits, going about his daily business, and he hits oil... "black gold"... "Texas tea."

But the herdsmen of Gerar quarreled with Isaac's herdsmen, saying, "The water is ours." So he called the name of the well Esek, because they quarreled with him. Then they dug another well, and they quarreled over that one also. So he called its name Sitnah. And he moved from there and dug another well, and they did not quarrel over it. So he called its name Rehoboth, because he said, "For now the LORD has made room for us, and we shall be fruitful in the land."

—GENESIS 26:20–22

The Philistines envied Isaac so much they kicked him out of Gerar, saying, "Oh, he's going to fail now. He's going to fall apart, and we don't need to worry about him anymore." The important fact is that even though they thought the blessing was upon the *place* where he was, the blessing was on his *obedience* to God.

To try to trip him up, the Philistines evicted him and were watching from behind a rock somewhere just hoping and waiting for him to fail. That's just like some people are waiting for your marriage to fall apart, for you to get laid off or laid up in an accident, for your business to go belly up, for you to file bankruptcy, for your car to be repossessed, or any number of other things to trip you up. The Philistines expected Isaac to wither away down there in the valley, but they were in for a surprise. A valley is just a low point between two high places. Although Isaac was in the low place of the valley, God was already planning his next high point!

So guess what Isaac did in the valley? He got some shovels and told his servants to start digging. All the while the Philistines are watching from over in the corner, snickering to themselves and waiting for him to fail. Instead of failure, they see water gushing up from where his servants had been digging! They must have wondered, *How come we didn't find that water?*

There is nowhere the devil can put you where God can't bless you! There is nowhere the devil can try to trap you where God can't reach you! You can get kicked out of Gerar and put in the valley, but if you stay in obedience, you will still be blessed!

Wells and Light

In the Gospels, light and water are often used as examples of the Spirit of Truth, the Holy Spirit. What would it be like if everywhere you set your foot, water and light gathered there? What if every time you opened a new location for your business, it was like one of those wells that Isaac dug? What if it was a place where people went to get their physical thirst quenched, but their spirits were touched as well? It is just like the woman who came to the well in John 4 and met Jesus.

Jesus said:

> You are the light of the world. A city that is set on a hill cannot be hidden. Nor do they light a lamp and put it under a basket, but on a lampstand, and it gives light to all who are in the house. Let your light so shine before men, that they may see your good works and glorify your Father in heaven.
>
> —Matthew 5:14–16

When Moses spent time in the presence of the Lord, his face shone so much that when he returned he had to put a veil over it so as not to startle the people of Israel. When is the last time the glory of God shone from your life so much that it startled someone? When was the last time you were prospering so much that the world was growing jealous, but at the same time clamoring to be with you so that you could reveal to them the secret of your success?

You know, the ministry has seen God do some great things in the last few years here in Orlando, but we have not arrived. God is not finished, so we are still pushing on! We are digging new wells and recharging our batteries in God's presence so that we can shine all the brighter. Our destiny is still out there, and we are not going to stop pursuing it!

Fourteen

God Blesses Us So
We Will Bless Others

I will bless you

And make your name great;

And you shall be a blessing.

—Genesis 12:2

GOD ALWAYS MEETS us where we are, but He also always expects us to grow. He is preparing the next step for us. In my life, and in the life of our church, He did this in an interesting way.

Even though we had closed a deal on the twenty-one acres with Faith World, I didn't have enough faith for building on it. By putting limitations on the big picture, I felt led to see what we could do about expanding the Powers Drive building to make it larger.

175

By then we had four services each Sunday and were overflowing for almost all of them. We simulcast through TV monitors in the gymnasium and set up chairs for more than two hundred people in there. By the latter half of 2000, we were running between twenty-five hundred and three thousand each Sunday. Souls were being saved, and members kept joining by the hundreds every month.

We felt quite loved by our neighbors, until we announced our desires to expand. Traffic was crazy on Powers Drive each Sunday, even with the police stepping in to help direct traffic as services transitioned. When our neighbors heard that we were thinking of building an addition to the sanctuary to seat an additional fifteen hundred people, they decided to try to block the plan. Every small complaint or slight grudge that someone had against us over the years came out at our first county commission hearing. People seemed to come out of the woodwork as if we were planning to build a strip joint or a brothel instead of a church. For the next several months, we ended up in a political struggle with the county commissioners to get the special zoning variance approval we needed to start construction on the expansion.

We went through several hearings, but by early 2001 we had finally received the approvals along the way that we needed to come before the Orange County commissioners for the final vote. Now, I had never gone through a process like this in Baltimore, so all of this was new to me. Throughout the process, I met a lot of community and county leaders I never would have crossed paths with otherwise. We hired a lobbyist to help us, who did a great job, and on the day of the final hearing I had three hundred T-shirts made for our supporters to wear in the county chambers so that our solidarity was evident. Our presentation that day went excellently, and despite the fact that our own area's commissioner voted against us, we carried the day four votes to three.

Then God pulled a fast one on me. He told me that instead of expanding the Powers building as we had just gotten permission to do, He wanted us to build on the twenty-one acres instead. All of the stress and work of the last few months had only been there to prepare us for what was ahead.

So in less than sixty days, because we already had drawings and building approvals through Faith World, we got the financing we needed. We began work on our present building around May of 2001. Little did I realize that we would need the new nineteen-hundred-seat auditorium before the building was even finished! By the time we moved into this new building in May of 2002, we had three thousand members, and more than two thousand showed up for our first service! It is a good thing we have learned over the years to keep lots of folding chairs around!

Today we are running three or four services a Sunday with about five thousand a week attending and about seventy-three hundred members. Our services are seen all over the world through television, and we are helping plant another church in Kissimmee, just south of Orlando. To be quite honest, I can't wait to see what God does next!

Coming Full Circle

In late 2003, I was again driving in my car (God seems to speak to me a lot when I am driving—perhaps because things are so busy now that driving is one of the only times my mind is quiet), and I heard the Holy Spirit say, "G Next." I thought about that for a moment, and He spoke again, "Generation Next." Then, in an instantaneous flash, I had a vision of a relay team running on a track, one runner passing the baton to the next, and again I heard the words, "Generation Next."

As I drove, the Holy Spirit began to explain that one relay runner represented one generation, and if that runner didn't successfully pass the baton to the next, the race could be lost. The practice and skill with which you passed that baton would determine how well you ran that race. I realized we would only get out what we put in. God was challenging me to build a facility solely dedicated to sowing into the next generation, the youth of our community.

Once I realized this, God led me down memory lane. As if through a slide show, I saw myself as a young teen on the corner of the arcade, meeting Marcus and the others for the first time; me running drugs and starting to sell; me starting to carry a gun and trying to kill Tony; me being shot at, getting arrested twice, getting locked up, going to forestry camp, and having that blowout with my dad. Then there was me buying drugs and starting to sell again, me strung out twenty-four/seven, and those horrible ghostly figures of my dream before I knelt in Doug's basement to accept Christ.

I knew there were kids in our area who were just like I had been—fatherless, impressionable, with no one to look up to but the guys on the corner selling drugs. I knew that if there were no godly images to help them find their destinies, they would only see the demonic ones set to crush their lives. I was convinced that God wanted me to build "a safe haven for the next generation" for the youth of our community.

Not only that, but God said we would do it all in cash—no loans at all, but the church would cover every payment on the building as it came due. As always, God was good to His word on this. Every dollar we needed to pay each month's draw from the construction company came in right on time.

So, in June of 2005, we opened our three-story youth facility that inlcudes a two-lane bowling alley, three full-court basketball courts, a full-service kitchen and dining area, an Internet café, an arcade with pool tables and Ping-Pong tables, and a thirty-five-hundred-square-foot fitness center for us "older" guys to use so that we can keep up with the young ones. About four hundred kids a week come through the facility, and the number continues to grow. While it is not overtly spiritual, we staff it with godly role models and pray before basketball games and in the arcade. We know as we continue to sow into the youth, we will reap a future harvest that will transform lives.

In addition to this, we continue to sow into the community so regularly that we don't even talk about needs from the pulpit anymore. Our outreaches on holidays are bigger than ever and include job fairs, doctors and dentists, toys, clothing, haircuts, services, and meals. In the last few years we have given away as many as forty-seven cars and helped with fifteen new home closings. As a result, lives continue to be changed, and our church continues to grow about a thousand members a year.

Seedtime and Harvest

A lot of people miss God's blessing for their lives because they don't recognize it when it comes. They are looking for the blessing to come fully grown and fruitful, but instead God just gives them the seed and waits to see what they do with it. If they just drop it and walk on, He has nothing to work with in their lives. However, if they plant it and start to nurture it until it grows, God will add His supernatural ability to their natural ability, and before long no one will be able to believe how big the tree is that grew from that tiny seed.

For me, the seed of destiny that was planted in my heart when I was born again has blossomed into a tree that bears fruit to feed thousands. No, I am not some great man with a greater calling than others; I am just a man with a great God who has made himself available to be a blessing to others. As a result, God took a drug dealer and a potential murderer and turned him into a pastor who is working to save the current and next generations from the fate Satan had planned for me. And I will tell you, there is no greater joy than being used by God in the special purpose He designed you for.

The world, however, does everything it can to distract us from this growth process of seed sprouting shoots, then the ear, and after that the full grains of corn in the ear. News and media channels focus on the overnight successes in sports and entertainment, particularly. The showier the better. Yet even overnight successes tend to come for people who have been working their gifts for a long time, only to finally spring to success. The tough years are always covered in a few seconds, however, and the luxuries that come from it take up the rest of the show.

But God does it all the other way around. Nothing comes to the world fully grown. All plants start with a seed. People start as seeds, also, grown into babies in the womb, and then come into the world needing parents to bring them to adulthood. Businesses start as ideas. Huge churches start with one person being called. Everything that God brings into the world, He brings in small so that the person nurturing and mentoring the seed will grow as the baby, business, career, or ministry grows.

Your destiny is small when you are given it to watch over, because you are inexperienced when you receive it. But you grow capable to handle each new level of its growth as you grow with it. If you don't, then both you and it fail. If you do, the world is changed through your success.

People miss this, though, because the blessing of God generally comes as an idea or a set of instructions to follow that don't necessarily make sense in the natural. Too often, the people being blessed disregard these instructions because they don't believe they will work. They get distracted by other things, or they never get over their own shortcomings enough to accept the blessing for what it is. Or they are too lazy to work to make it grow, or any number of other reasons that keep them from believing in and activating the destiny God has for them.

The command, the demand, or the idea that God speaks into your heart for your blessing will not check with your convenience, either. In fact, it is almost sure to shake you out of your comfort zone. It will challenge you. God's blessings are not about living the easy life—they are about living the purposeful life of making your destiny a reality and your world a better place for you having been in it.

God's dreams are always bigger than anything you can accomplish on your own. Too many people claim the next level with their lips, but they aren't willing to make the necessary changes to go to that level or to travel through the wilderness that will get them there. For example, we may not be willing to forgive the very person who is the key to our success, just because that person hurt us in the past and we don't want to let go of the grudge. Maybe there is a part of our personality that needs to change before we can gather the team needed to accomplish the dream. Perhaps there is more fruit of the Spirit needed before we can start. Perhaps we need a more disciplined, scheduled time every day in the Word and in prayer. It might be any number of things, but chances are it is a step we are capable of taking, although we may resist it because it is inconvenient or uncomfortable.

This is why your life has not changed even though you quote twenty scriptures a day. You may know every prosperity scripture in the Bible, but prosperity has yet to visit you because you have not yet followed the secret of the power to get wealth that is locked into the idea God has already laid on your heart. Or you may be living for the blessings instead of pursuing the Blesser. It is obeying that command or idea from God that will produce the results that will blow your mind, but you are missing it because you are looking for an easier road. You may even be ignoring God's Word to you in the Bible, hoping for some supernatural revelation. But it will never come if God can't trust you to know—and live—what He already told you to do in Scripture.

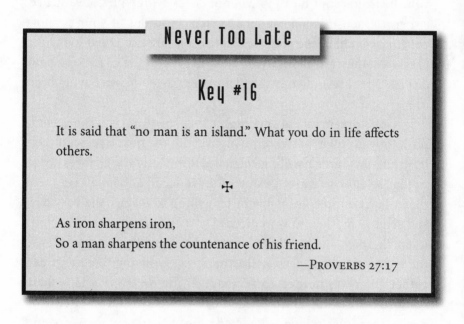

Never Too Late

Key #16

It is said that "no man is an island." What you do in life affects others.

✠

As iron sharpens iron,
So a man sharpens the countenance of his friend.

—PROVERBS 27:17

Some of you are mad and bitter that others are prospering, but you are not obeying what God has put in your heart to do or His Word! You can't ever allow yourself to get bored with obeying the commands of the Bible!

The power to succeed in your destiny is locked in an idea or a command that will make a demand on your faith. Look at how it happened for Abraham:

Now the LORD had said to Abram:

Fifteen

Rejoice!
You Are on Your Way

Do not sorrow, for the joy of the LORD is
your strength.

—Nehemiah 8:10

IN GENESIS 25, the Bible begins the story of twin brothers Jacob
and Esau. There are a number of parallels we can draw from this
story to what we have discussed about how to find God's destiny
for your life.

In speaking to Rebekah about her sons, God revealed that
heaven's perspective is often quite different than our own:

Now Isaac pleaded with the LORD for his wife, because she was
barren; and the LORD granted his plea, and Rebekah his wife
conceived. But the children struggled together within her; and

she said, "If all is well, why am I like this?" So she went to inquire of the LORD. And the LORD said to her:

"Two nations are in your womb,
Two peoples shall be separated from your body;
One people shall be stronger than the other,
And the older shall serve the younger."

—GENESIS 25:21–23

Rebekah was carrying twins, and they were fighting inside of her. They were struggling inside of her to such an extent that she couldn't sleep at night. She was up all day, up all night because she kept feeling the bouncing and turmoil inside, but she couldn't see what was causing it. So she went to the Lord concerning the situation.

Learn to Use God's Sonogram

God has a different kind of sonogram than the one your hospital has. All the hospital can tell you is whether it is a healthy boy or a girl. You can't use regular or natural vision to see what is ahead. If you don't learn how to look through the sonogram of heaven, you will not know how to move correctly in life. You have to learn how to see as the Lord sees. You have to pray, "Lord, change my vision." That is why sometimes you can't even drive straight home from work—you have got to go through a new community to increase your expectations. You just have to go out and look at new houses. Sometimes you have to stop by a car dealership. Why? Because you need a bigger vision. You need to remember that there are bigger and better things out there.

Too often we are limited by what we have now, and God is trying to get us to take the blinders off. He is trying to switch us from a deficit mentality to an abundance mentality. In order for you to accomplish all He wants you to accomplish, He has to increase your level of expectation, because your expectation determines your impartation. If God sends you a blessing, and you are too narrow-minded to recognize it for what it is—just like I was the first time God sent that man to pay off my debt—then you could miss what God is trying to do for you! You are too focused on your problems, and God is trying to get you open to your destiny!

From before we are born, God impregnates each of us with a vision of our destiny, but at the same time the devil tries to deceive us with a false vision of identity and the limitations of this world. From the time these two visions are conceived, they are fighting against one another. They are twins, so they can look exactly alike on the outside but be completely different on the inside. The world system will say that identity is the way—just as tradition at the time Rebekah was pregnant was that the younger brother would serve the older. But God doesn't see it that way. God says that the world system has it backward, and, in this case, the lineage of Abraham would go through the younger twin, not the older. Your future, and that of your children, must be based on fulfilling your God-given destiny. It cannot be based on matching what the world calls success, or, worse, upon being defeated by the world's system, which is poised to keep us discontented, disillusioned, and in despair.

When God looked at Rebekah's sons, He didn't see two boys, two neighborhoods, two counties, or two states—He saw *two nations*. He looked into her womb and saw the potential of those two boys already played out for the next several millennia. He sees generation after generation of destiny fulfilled and what that can mean to the world. He sees possibilities, dreams, aspirations, and purpose. God has big plans for each of us, and when He looks at you He sees anything but a failure.

Be Careful to Whom You Tell Your Dream

Be careful to whom you tell your dream, because once you start seeing what God sees in you, what you say will sound crazy to everyone else. It could cause you more trouble than good. Look at what happened to Joseph. He had a dream from God that he told his family about, and they hated him for it. They wanted to kill him, but settled for selling him off to Egypt! Joseph saw through the telescope of heaven, and he saw the right thing, but his problem wasn't his dream; it was his mouth. He told too many people.

Don't tell people what God is going to do through you. Just let God do what He is going to do! Meditate on it, pray about it, let God reveal all of the details of it to your heart—but don't talk big because you want to impress people, be popular, and hang out with the in-crowd. No, just let God do it! You don't have to tell anybody anything!

But even if you have slipped up, God is still big enough to make it all happen. Even though Joseph was persecuted and locked up, he kept a good attitude and hung on to his vision. Thirteen years later, he went from the outhouse to the White House in a day. He was still successful; he still lived his dream, but it might have been a much easier road had he not gone around shooting his mouth off!

People who are comfortable where they are in mediocrity have a hard time dealing with visionaries. If you start talking about your dreams, they might attack you! "Oh, Cici, honey, you know that can't happen." "Oh, Billy-boy, you know you can't do that. You gonna be in the projects forever!" But I am here to tell you that the devil is a liar! You don't have to listen to what they tell you—you just have to get hold of the voice of God and obey it no matter what the world around you says to stop you.

Send a message to heaven and hell. Tell heaven that you expect something great. And tell hell, "You ain't going to keep me much longer." The very fact that you are experiencing a tough time is evidence that God knows you can handle it. He won't let you go through troubles without the assurance that you have what it takes to learn from them and to be stronger for it on the other side.

If you are going through it now, God is preparing you for a step up. The success members in my congregation and I have had by applying what I am teaching you in these pages is proof to you that God's ways work best! Seek God's voice, obey it, and be ready for the tests. God already sees what you can become—don't sell yourself short. God has no small plans!

Perseverance is a key for you just as it was for Joseph. God will shake things up, and if you are not careful, when God is shaking things up, it will scare you. Don't get scared by the shaking. The shaking may be necessary because you have become too comfortable where you are. God either has to accept that you will be less than you could be, or He has to make it inconvenient to stay where you are. So out of His love for you, which do you think He will do? Which would you do for your son or daughter?

You see, after a while every baby that is inside of a woman's womb starts sending messages: "I gotta get out! The place where I am is too small for me. This can't hold my destiny. It was a good incubator, but it can't hold me forever. I need a bigger space so that I can grow up and do more than just swim around in a warm pool being fed by someone else." Could it be any different with the destinies inside of us?

The Bible says that while Rebekah was giving birth, Esau came out first. I don't know how, but Jacob must have heard the conversation, because Jacob says, "This doesn't look like what God said. If I am going to be the blessed one, I should be the first one out, because that is the normal order." And Jacob reaches his hand out— normally the head comes out first—and grabs his brother's leg, trying to pull him back or trip him up.

There was a problem. Logically, Esau should have the birthright. But God said that the younger was going to end up with the blessing, and the older was going to serve the younger. This is where too many in the kingdom of God fall into error, just as Jacob did: They hear the prophecy...they hear the promises...they see God's vision for themselves, and they think *they* have to make it happen. So they fall into the world's ways to do the work of God. Like Jacob, they begin scheming and conniving to get to their destined place. They play games and try to politic themselves into places of authority and power. If you keep doing that, you won't reach your destiny!

Jacob started playing games just like that, thinking that he had to trick his way to the top. The story in Genesis tells us that Jacob tricked his brother out of his birthright when he was hungry, and then he went into the tent of his father and tricked Isaac out of the blessing he intended for Esau.

Jacob resorted to scheming and conniving to get to the top, but I will tell you that if you want to do it that way, you had better watch your back when you start to succeed! If you pushed other people down and stepped on them to climb the ladder—if you cut others down, gossiped, backstabbed, and sabotaged your way up— you won't be up there long. And while you are up there, you won't enjoy it, because you will spend all your time trying to stay there and fend off the other backstabbers and saboteurs. You won't have any time to enjoy it, nor will you be able to accomplish any of the great things God called you to that place to do, either.

Jacob was destined for greatness. He was a prince, but he lived as a crook. As a result, he became a fugitive. He was living "on the down-low." He was living "an alternative lifestyle." He had something going on behind the scene. But Jacob had it wrong. He thought he had to make God's prophecy come true himself, so he became a trickster and con man. He missed it in the same way we do if we think we have to claw our way to the top to realize our destinies.

We certainly have to have a fighter's mentality if we are going to make it to the top, and we definitely need the tenacity of a pit bull. But we need to fight God's way and be tenacious to His Word. We are not here to fight others or put others down so we can use them as steps to where God wants us to go. God isn't calling us to be connivers or schemers. He wants us to be servants who say, "I am going to be everything that God wants me to be!" Refuse to compromise. True promotion only comes from God. We are going to put on the armor, but He is going to fight the battles. It is our part to obey His commands, and He will bring the victory!

How are you living? "God gave me a dream." Yeah... well, how is God going to promote you into your destiny while you are still playing games? You are destined to be a prince or princess, but God will not promote a mess. *God can't bless no mess.*

Embrace the vision that is your destiny. Hold tight to it, but let God promote you into its fulfillment. God doesn't make any mistakes. Just as Mary did when the angel spoke to her, we need to be ready to obey God's request that we give birth to what He has placed in us.

> Then Mary said to the angel, "How can this be, since I do not know a man?" And the angel answered and said to her, "The Holy Spirit will come upon you, and the power of the Highest will overshadow you; therefore, also, that Holy One who is to be born will be called the Son of God. Now indeed, Elizabeth your relative has also conceived a son in her old age; and this is now the sixth month for her who was called barren. For with God nothing will be impossible." Then Mary said, "Behold the maidservant of the Lord! Let it be to me according to your word." And the angel departed from her.
>
> —Luke 1:34–38

God came to Mary, and all Mary had was one question: "How are You going to do this thing? I haven't had sex; tell me how You are going to do this."

God responded to her question by saying, "I am going to overshadow you, and My power is going to be enough to impregnate you."

Mary's simple response was, "Let it be as Your Word says." Mary had what they call the *immaculate conception*. All she did was take God at His Word.

God wants you to move on this truth, because He has your destiny waiting for you. Visualize where God wants you to go. Then there is nothing left but to act on your faith.

Enjoy the Journey

It's not how you started the race; it is how you finish it. But knowing what you know now, not only should you be able to finish well, but you also should be able to enjoy the rest of the race.

In the midst of some of his greatest trials, Paul offered some interesting advice. He wrote his letter to the Philippians from a Roman prison cell, and in one of the shortest books of the Bible he tells them twelve times to rejoice.

How can he say this? Look at the advice he offers:

Rejoice in the Lord always. Again I will say, rejoice! Let your gentleness be known to all men. The Lord is at hand. Be anxious for nothing, but in everything by prayer and supplication, with thanksgiving, let your requests be made known to God; and the peace of God, which surpasses all understanding, will guard your hearts and minds through Christ Jesus.

Finally, brethren, whatever things are true, whatever things are noble, whatever things are just, whatever things are pure, whatever things are lovely, whatever things are of good report, if there is any virtue and if there is anything praiseworthy—meditate on these things. The things which you learned and received and heard and saw in me, these do, and the God of peace will be with you.

But I rejoiced in the Lord greatly that now at last your care for me has flourished again; though you surely did care, but you lacked opportunity. Not that I speak in regard to need, for I have learned in whatever state I am, to be content: I know how to be abased, and I know how to abound. Everywhere and in all things I have learned both to be full and to be hungry, both to abound and to suffer need. I can do all things through Christ who strengthens me.

—Philippians 4:4–13

Paul's message here is simple: If I have Jesus and am doing what He has instructed me to do, no matter what the circumstances look like, I have everything I need and can be content. If I have an anxiety, all I have to do is pray and praise God for the answer. If bad things happen, I have the goodness of God and what He has done for me in the past to think about. In all things I can have His peace, because I know I am in His hands.

What can I add to that? Wherever you are today in your journey on the road to your destiny, rejoice! God is with you. Enjoy the trip and the scenery. Encourage one another with testimonies of what God has done. Do what He gives you to do, and be content with whatever you have now, because however little or much it is, it is enough if you put it in Jesus' hands—let Him bless it and make it multiply.

Jesus Is Coming!

In Mark chapter 5, the Bible tells the story of Jairus, a father and a religious leader who comes to Jesus to ask, "My little daughter lies at the point of death. Come and lay Your hands on her, that she may be healed, and she will live" (v. 23). Jesus agreed, and they left for Jairus's home. I want you to realize today that if you have asked Jesus to come, He is on His way to your house to deal with your dark and ugly situation as well.

However, the Bible says that along the way, among the crowds thronging around Him, someone reached out and touched Jesus. It was a woman with an issue of blood who had come to touch Him and be healed. At this Jesus stopped to talk with her and help her further. He was distracted, but He didn't change his mind about going to Jairus's house; he was only delayed on the way there.

Today, your blessing may be delayed in a similar way. Your breakthrough may be delayed. Your healing or your promotion may be delayed, but it cannot be denied. You need to remember that Jesus is on the way. He is coming. And if you see others around you getting their breakthroughs or miracles, don't grow jealous; rejoice! It is only more proof that Jesus is near you and on the way to your house as well.

Even if, like Jairus, you hear the situation is hopeless, don't despair. When Jairus stood there waiting while Jesus ministered to the woman with the issue of blood, servants came from his house to say, "Your daughter is dead. Why trouble the Teacher any further?" (v. 35). But it was not too late. It is never too late. Jesus turned to Jairus and told him what to do: "Do not be afraid. Only believe" (v. 36).

We need to heed that advice as well. Jesus didn't change His mind; He was still on the way to Jairus's house to heal his daughter. Because of the woman with the issue of blood, it took a little longer, but that didn't make any difference to Jesus. He didn't change His mind. He was still the Son of God. He was still the Healer. He was still answering Jairus's request to Him. Remember, it is never too late.

Never Too Late

Key #17

It's not how you start the race; it's how you finish it. Stay the course to destiny.

☩

But none of these things move me; nor do I count my life dear to myself, so that I may finish my race with joy, and the ministry which I received from the Lord Jesus, to testify to the gospel of the grace of God.

—ACTS 20:24

Remember, when Jesus heard Lazarus was dying, He didn't worry. He didn't hurry. It was four days before He showed up in Bethany, and Lazarus was already three days in the tomb. His body was already decaying, but that didn't matter to Jesus. His miracle power was still as strong as ever, and it took only three words from Jesus to raise Lazarus back up again. He intentionally waited so that there could be no mistaking the miracle. Remember, it is never too late!

You may say, "Yeah, but you are so blessed, preacher! You have no idea what it is like to wait so long! Jesus can't be coming anymore! I am better off quitting!" Believe it or not, I know how you feel. I am still waiting on miracles myself, but I am not giving up! For me, God has already answered a lot of His promises to me, a big part of my destiny is already being fulfilled, but there are still places where I am waiting on God. My son has been diagnosed with cerebral palsy, and I am still waiting on his healing. But I know it is coming. Jesus is still on His way, and every time I see a miracle in my congregation, I know He is one step closer to getting to my son. I'm believing and professing it. I have laid hands on him and confessed the Word over him. So we are waiting and anticipating God's arrival. The Bible tells us, "Let us hold fast the profession of our faith without wavering; (for he is faithful that promised;)" (Heb. 10:23, KJV). We cannot waver. We are waiting with a spirit of anticipation.

In the parable of the prodigal son, how do you think the father saw his son coming back to him except that he was expecting him? He would stand at that window every day, watching the road for his son's return. The Bible doesn't say how long that son was gone, but we know the father waited. Every day he would watch out that window waiting for his son's return. He never gave up on the restoration of his son back into fellowship with his family.

Keep watching out the window. Jesus is still on the way! It's never too late.

You need to know it is never too late. It's not too late right now, no matter what the doctor said, no matter what the lawyer said, no matter what your husband or wife said, no matter what the school said, no matter what the mortgage lender said. It's not too late. Jesus is coming!

If you are doing all that you have learned to do in this book, rejoice; you are on your way to your destiny. Enjoy every step of the journey, because Jesus *is* coming!

Conclusion

Never Too Late Key #1

You must learn to see yourself through the telescope of heaven to see what God sees. Spiritual eyesight is more important than natural vision.

✠

Eye has not seen, nor ear heard,
Nor have entered into the heart of man
The things which God has prepared for those who love Him.

—1 Corinthians 2:9

Never Too Late Key #2

God is able to use the failure of your past as fertilizer for your future.

✠

And we know that all things work together for good to those who love God, to those who are the called according to His purpose.

—Romans 8:28

Never Too Late Key #3

The people you hang with become a prophecy of your future. Who is in your circle of influence?

✠

My son, do not walk in the way with them,
Keep your foot from their path;
For their feet run to evil,
And they make haste to shed blood....
They lie in wait for their own blood,
They lurk secretly for their own lives.

—Proverbs 1:15–16, 18

Never Too Late Key #4

The best setup is a God setup! Say *yes* when He makes an offer you can't refuse.

✠

How long, you simple ones, will you love simplicity?
For scorners delight in their scorning,
And fools hate knowledge.
Turn at my rebuke;
Surely I will pour out my spirit on you;
I will make my words known to you....
Whoever listens to me will dwell safely,
And will be secure, without fear of evil.

—Proverbs 1:22–23, 33

Never Too Late Key #5

In life, you have two choices, *right* or *wrong*—there's not much left in the middle, and eventually you will have to choose.

✝

I call heaven and earth as witnesses today against you, that I have set before you life and death, blessing and cursing; therefore choose life, that both you and your descendants may live.

—DEUTERONOMY 30:19

Never Too Late Key #6

Rottenness deteriorates and eats away the tissue until it dies. Filthiness is surface dirt that can be washed off. You can choose to die or be washed clean.

✝

There is therefore now no condemnation to those who are in Christ Jesus, who do not walk according to the flesh, but according to the Spirit. For the law of the Spirit of life in Christ Jesus has made me free from the law of sin and death.

—ROMANS 8:1–2

Never Too Late Key #7

Diamonds are found hidden under thick layers of black coal deep within the earth. Your true wealth is hidden deep within you as well.

✝

The kingdom of God does not come with observation; nor will they say, "See here!" or "See there!" For indeed, the kingdom of God is within you.

—LUKE 17:20–21

Never Too Late Key #8

The growth of a plant depends on its root system, on being planted in good soil, and on being given water and light. There is a seed in you that needs to grow.

✠

Grow in the grace and knowledge of our Lord and Savior Jesus Christ.

—2 PETER 3:18

Never Too Late Key #9

Seek the wisdom of God for man, not man for the wisdom of God.

✠

Get wisdom! Get understanding!
Do not forget, nor turn away from the words of my mouth.
Do not forsake her, and she will preserve you;
Love her, and she will keep you.
Wisdom is the principal thing;
Therefore get wisdom.

—PROVERBS 4:5–7

Never Too Late Key #10

In the Old Testament days, they strapped small, lighted candles to their ankles to light their way in the darkness of night to prevent them from stumbling over rocks or treading on snakes. The Word of God is a lamp that illuminates your pathway in life.

✝

Your word is a lamp to my feet
And a light to my path.

—PSALM 119:105

Never Too Late Key #11

Change is not change until you change. A seed stays a seed if it resists change.

✝

To everything there is a season,
A time for every purpose under heaven.

—ECCLESIASTES 3:1

Never Too Late Key #12

When a farmer gathers his corn in the fall season, some of it is saved to plant in the spring season. Save your seed that will bring you another harvest season.

✝

Now may He who supplies seed to the sower, and bread for food, supply and multiply the seed you have sown and increase the fruits of your righteousness, while you are enriched in everything for all liberality, which causes thanksgiving through us to God.

—2 CORINTHIANS 9:10–11

Never Too Late Key #13

A waiter serves you with great service because he knows he'll get a great tip. Serving God has a greater reward than a good tip.

✠

Knowing that whatever good anyone does, he will receive the same from the Lord, whether he is a slave or free.

—EPHESIANS 6:8

Never Too Late Key #14

A successful entrepreneur gains more wealth because he knows the principle of investing. When you invest in the work of God, you are making a deposit in the bank of heaven. When you need a withdrawal, it will be there.

✠

Honor the LORD with your possessions,
And with the firstfruits of all your increase;
So your barns will be filled with plenty,
And your vats will overflow with new wine.

—PROVERBS 3:9–10

Never Too Late Key #15

You only pursue what you have not obtained. Start s-t-r-e-t-c-h-i-n-g!

✠

I press toward the goal for the prize of the upward call of God in Christ Jesus.

—PHILIPPIANS 3:14

Other Products by Zachery Tims

3-D Vision Pack
Tape $15   CD $20   DVD $30

Dr. Zachery Tims offers a God-perspective with this prolific 3-D message series preached from Bishop T. D. Jakes' Potter's House. This series includes: "Divine Reversal," "Don't Let Your Past Rob You of Your Dreams," and "Outlast Your Storm." If God hasn't done it already, get ready, He's going to flip the script.

Another Spirit
Tape $15   CD $20   DVD $30

Numbers 14:24 tells us that because Caleb had another spirit in him and followed God fully, God brought him into the land promised to Caleb and his descendants. Do you want to walk into the land God has promised to you? Listen as Dr. Zachery Tims illuminates what it takes to have the "Caleb spirit."

Back to the Basics
Tape $15   CD $20   DVD $30

In this three-part series, Dr. Zachery Tims takes us back to the basics. As you apply these truths to your everyday living, expect God to propel you into new dimensions of your Christian walk.

Delay Is Not Denial
Tape $10   CD $15   DVD $20

Your promises may seem delayed, but never forget that they haven't been denied! As you line up with God's Word, you can be sure that it's just a matter of time before His promises are manifested in your life.

Empowered for Success
Tape $20   CD $25   DVD $40

God's commanded blessings for your life! He has a land flowing with blessings for you without measure. Get ready to be empowered for success

Fight Back!
Tape $15   CD $20   DVD $30

Does it seem like the enemy has been pushing you around? Fight back! Put on the whole armor of God, take up the weapons of your warfare, and fight back!

Fruit of Spirit Vol. 5: Faith—Part 1
Tape $20   CD $25   DVD $40

Without faith, it is impossible to please God. Faith is a fruit of the Spirit that propels us to pursue God's promises relentlessly. Walk according to faith, and you will overcome obstacles!

Fruit of Spirit Vol. 5: Faith—Part 2
Tape $20   CD $25   DVD $40

Dr. Zachery Tims continues this Faith series with encouraging messages: "Crazy Faith," "Faith for the Family," "Now Faith," and "Increase My Faith."

Get Up, Get Out, Get Down
Tape $15   CD $20   DVD $30

In this dynamic, three-part series, Dr. Zachery Tims delivers the motivating message: "Get Up, Get Out and Get Down." Get up from where you are. Get out of the places from where God is moving you. And, get down to God's promised land of provision and prosperity for you!

I'm a Survivor
Tape $20   CD $25   DVD $40

Do you feel like you are fighting battles that you cannot win? Well, this dynamic series of messages will bring out the fighter in you! No matter what your situation is, by the time you're finished getting these messages into your spirit, you'll be shouting, "I'M A SURVIVOR. I'M NOT GOING TO GIVE UP!"

New Levels, New Devils
Tape $20   CD $25   DVD $40

Climbing to new levels in God will cause you to encounter demonic opposition that you haven't faced before. After all, this is a turf war! But allow Dr. Zachery and Pastor Riva Tims to equip you to war this warfare skillfully and effectively. Swat the fly!

Pursuing Excellence
Tape $25   CD $35   DVD $50

Excellence is the attention to detail that produces superior results. Are you pursuing excellence in your life? Does every area of your life model excellence? In this five-part series, Dr. Zachery Tims coaches us that excellence is progressive and comes with persecution and a price. How much can God trust you with?

Real-ationships Vol. 1: The 3 Cs
Tape $15   CD $20   DVD $30

It's time to take off your mask and get real about making your marriage better and stronger! This series will help you establish the fundamental building blocks for a successful marriage: understanding roles within a marriage, effective communication, and conflict resolution.

Real-ationships Vol. 2: Built to Last
Tape $15   CD $20   DVD $30

Marriages should be built to last. Divorce was never God's plan for our marriages. Dr. Zachery and Pastor Riva Tims designed this series to retrain your thinking and give you the tools to build a marriage that will stand the tests of time.

Real-ationships Vol. 3: Let's Talk About Sex
Tape $10   CD $15   DVD $20

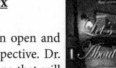

This is the series that you've been waiting for—an open and honest discussion about sex, from a biblical perspective. Dr. Zachery and Pastor Riva Tims provide instructions that will help you make intimacy a way of life and not just a five-minute occurrence.

Whatsoever You Say
Tape $15   CD $20   DVD $30

You have the power to frame your world with your words. Both your victory and defeat live in your mouth! It is God's desire that we would use our mouths as weapons to defeat the enemy.

When You Pray
Tape $10   CD $15   DVD $20

Nothing happens until you pray! When you pray according to God's will, God hears you. And, you can be confident that you will see His hand move in due season. But, it's not until you pray.